Playwrights for Tomorrow

VOLUME 9

Encore

BY DAVID KORR

Madam Popov

BY GLADDEN SCHROCK

Children of the Kingdom

BY THE COMPANY THEATRE ENSEMBLE
WITH SCRIPT BY DON KEITH OPPER

Psalms of Two Davids

BY JOEL SCHWARTZ

EDITED, WITH AN INTRODUCTION, BY ARTHUR H. BALLET

PLAYWRIGHTS FOR TOMORROW

A Collection of Plays, Volume 9

THE UNIVERSITY OF MINNESOTA PRESS   •   MINNEAPOLIS

Printed in the United States of America at
North Central Publishing Co., St. Paul

Library of Congress Catalog Card Number: 66-19124

ISBN 0-8166-0653-6

PUBLISHED IN THE UNITED KINGDOM AND INDIA BY OXFORD UNIVERSITY PRESS, LONDON AND DELHI, AND IN CANADA BY THE COPP CLARK PUBLISHING CO. LIMITED, TORONTO

These volumes of *Playwrights for Tomorrow*
are respectfully and lovingly dedicated to
the late Sir Tyrone Guthrie — a friend, an
inspiration, and a very great man
of the theatre.

Playwrights for Tomorrow

VOLUME 9

INTRODUCTION

Arthur H. Ballet

As Sabina in Thornton Wilder's *Skin of Our Teeth* says: "Oh — why can't we have plays like we used to have — *Peg o' My Heart*, and *Smilin' Thru*, and *The Bat* . ." Well, Sabina, we still do have plays like that. Playwrights write them and theatres do them. Despite protests to the contrary, I rather suspect that writers, audiences, and theatres really do want "plays like we used to have . . good entertainment with a message you can take home with you!"

The Office for Advanced Drama Research (O.A.D.R.) has tried to find new voices and daring theatres to produce the different plays. The O.A.D.R. was established in 1963 at the University of Minnesota, with financial aid from the Rockefeller Foundation, to provide an opportunity for playwrights seeking to try fresh paths, an opportunity to have their work performed without the pressures endemic to the commercial theatre. At first productions were limited to the Minneapolis–St. Paul area, but the program was expanded in 1969 and since then productions have been staged under O.A.D.R. aegis in many parts of the country.

It takes a steady hand to run the O.A.D.R. program. After reading literally thousands of unproduced plays during the several years of directing the O.A.D.R., I'm not so sure my hand is nearly as sure as it used to be. I'm shaken to find myself now reading imitation Megan Terry, Terrence McNally, Sam Shepard, Jean-Claude van Itallie, Maria Irene Fornés, and Rochelle Owens. It seems only last week I was trying to get theatres to take a fling with those writers, and now would-be playwrights are imitating them.

Stranger still to have some of the very theatres which rejected those "famous" playwrights seven years ago when I sent their work to them now returning to me new work by others with testy little notes reminding me of their interest only in quality work such as that of Megan Terry. The world does whirl.

Strangest perhaps of all to read the directors' rejections of the new scripts sent to them. Their criticism tends to lament the lack of "style" in our native writers. (The assumption here is that only the British can really write anyway.) Or they condemn the "inept theatre sense" of the playwrights of today. Or they inform me that they are really looking for "experimentation." I shudder in disbelief when I see the stage work of those very critical directors. If the new writers are somewhat lacking (and indeed they may be), so are the directors themselves. They too sometimes fall short of "style" and "theatre sense" and even a smidgen of theatrical daring. But *they* have the theatres, and playwrights need their theatres — whereas directors, incompetent or otherwise, don't really need living playwrights.

Is it any wonder that I often question my skill at the delicate task of finding playwrights and theatres which can somehow come together effectively, with the generous financial assistance of the Rockefeller Foundation as administered by the University of Minnesota. Fortunately, though, there are just enough theatres willing and able to take a chance and enough writers creatively exploring the world around them to make the work exciting and even stabilizing — some of the time.

The plays and playwrights in these two simultaneously issued volumes, numbers 8 and 9, of *Playwrights for Tomorrow* are a mixed bag in every way: young and old, experienced and inexperienced, collegiate and professional, and small as well as large in endeavor, in scope, in passion, and in vision. But of the thousands I've read and the scores we've managed to get staged, these works more or less represent where the action seems to be at the moment.

Yale Udoff's *A Gun Play* went the whole route for the O.A.D.R. After I had read it and sent it to a number of theatres, Paul Weidner of the Hartford Stage Company had the great good sense to be struck by the potential of the play. He staged it most successfully in Connecticut, where commercial producers optioned the play after the *New York Times* critic Mel Gussow had commended it. These producers eventually brought it to New York City for an off-Broadway run which raised hackles in some quarters and high praise in others. Clive Barnes, also of the *Times*, proclaimed its importance and loyally supported the play through a precarious run. Udoff, a professional writer primarily involved in the mass media, probably has turned an important corner in his career and for the theatre.

Chiefly a professional actor in film and television, Allen Joseph turned to playwriting in the midst of a well-established career in the theatre. The result, *Anniversary on Weedy Hill*, is clearly a work for the theatre. Produced by Theatre West, a company of earnest and dedicated professionals in West Hollywood, the play had an excellent cast and was itself funny, true, honest, and very affecting on stage — as it is in reading. One unusual note: about a year after this production, one of the actors in *Anniversary on Weedy Hill*, Hal Lynch, wrote a play himself and it was presented, again with support from the O.A.D.R., at — of all places — Theatre West.

The Nihilist by William N. Monson was the second play the O.A.D.R. offered through the facilities of the University of California at Davis Theatre under the direction of Alfred Rossi. And once again this academic theatre brought a vitality and an immediacy to a play drawing richly on history. Monson, himself from the world of academe, benefited from Rossi's theatrical staging of the play — which burst the physical confines of the theatre. The play here published reflects that learning and that sense of what a play can achieve in a theatre.

David Korr's *Encore* and Gladden Schrock's *Madam Popov* were originally scheduled as a double bill at the Other Place Theatre of The Tyrone Guthrie Theater in Minneapolis, but the director and company so enjoyed working with the individual writers that eventually the evenings were expanded, and each playwright's work was performed as a separate entity. The 1970 season at the Guthrie was sadly lackluster — except for the work of the Other Place Theatre's young company and these two writers. A number of pleasantly unprejudiced individuals indicated that Korr and Schrock provided the best theatre in town that summer — and certainly I'll agree.

Children of the Kingdom by Don Keith Opper is the result of close cooperation between playwright, company, and director. The Company Theatre in Los Angeles and its gifted, imaginative director, Steven Kent, nurtured the concept with Opper and together they made exciting, incisive theatre. The O.A.D.R.'s function was simply to encourage a very young and creative writer and to aid his theatre in realizing that potential.

In considering Joel Schwartz's work I admit bias: a few years ago he was a graduate student working under my direction at the University of

Minnesota. An earlier play, written at Minnesota and produced successfully there and at the Mark Taper Forum in Los Angeles, bore the promise of an important talent. *Psalm of Two Davids*, though, struck me as a major breakthrough for this writer and for playwriting generally. It pointed a new direction: almost neoclassic in form and yet reflecting a kind of mysticism and spaced-out insight, this work was rejected by dozens of theatres — for one reason or another. Finally, Jim Dunn at the College of Marin in California read it and flipped. His production at the two-year college was, without much doubt, one of the most impressive productions of any play in the O.A.D.R.'s repertory. A mixed audience packed the theatre night after night and accorded the play a standing ovation. In addition to providing a first-rank writer with a first-rank production, this experience disproved old fears about new plays at tiny schools. But then of course not many small schools have Jim Dunns directing their productions — indeed, lamentably very few large schools have Jim Dunns, either.

As these volumes go off to the printer, the future of the O.A.D.R. is unpredictable. The plays continue to arrive, and I read them all. The theatres continue to say they want to do new plays, and I try to help find them, but I sometimes think they really want *King Lear* or *Smilin' Through*. And the writers are quite often represented by literary agents who set up impossible — not to say stupid — barriers to production. The Rockefeller Foundation is thinking about trying other ways to help playwrights, and so is the O.A.D.R. Meanwhile, my own hand now and then feels a shade less steady than it used to feel. Even as the trembling begins, though, I know it's been worth it. I hope the reader — and the producer — agree. Theatre is little more than a shaky stab in the dark that sometimes strikes magnificent sparks. We try.

DAVID KORR

Encore

A SHORT PLAY FOR THREE VOICES AND GUITAR

for the few

Cast of Characters

SETH
BENNY
OLD MAN

ENCORE

The curtains remain closed; from behind them steps a man with a broom. His name is Seth and he is middle-aged and ill-tempered. He begins to sweep halfheartedly, then notices the audience.

SETH

Oh Jesus, not again. (*He looks around the audience without a grain of curiosity, and clucks to himself.*) Hey, Benny!

BENNY

(*from backstage*) What's that?

SETH

C'mere.

BENNY

(*looking out from behind the curtains*) Hello?

SETH

They're back.

BENNY

Well, I'll be damned. Persistent bunch, aren't they. (*He comes out.*)

SETH

Somebody must have sold tickets for every night the theatre's closed. Made himself a little pocket money. People don't bother to check. They just come when the ticket says come. They must not have read last night's reviews.

BENNY

Boy, that crowd was mad. Thought we'd never get rid of them. But no fussing tonight. You tell them straight out there's nothing on till next week. Send them home.

SETH

I don't know that we ought to. Anybody complains, we're in trouble. Some of them pay as much as a dollar and a half to sit out there.

BENNY

Much as that you reckon? Well, let them sit then. I don't mind. Long as they don't bother us.

SETH

No, we've got to fix them up with something. They don't look as easy as the tourists last night.

BENNY

Well, old Pastrami, or whatever his name is, is back there.

SETH

Who?

BENNY

The old gent that plays the guitar. You've seen him. With the white hair, wears old-fashioned suits, always nodding to himself. Used to give concerts here a long time back.

SETH

What's he doing here now?

BENNY

Doorman lets him in. Remembers him from forty years ago. The old fellow's harmless enough. He comes in and sort of sifts through his memories. He's on the stage right now with an old guitar, parked on that load of props they're using next week. He's just sitting, playing quietly to himself.

SETH

Is he any good?

BENNY

I suppose. They say he was famous.

SETH

Well, he's the best we got. I hope he's in good form. C'mon, let's catch him in the act. You get the curtains and I'll put the lights on him. (*They disappear. In a moment the curtain goes up very quietly, in fits and starts. Suddenly spotlights come on and reveal an old man sitting forlornly among a pile of props and stage furniture, bent over a stringless guitar. When he realizes the lights are on, he hugs the guitar to himself, and, squinting, peers out into the audience. Seth comes on from the wings, still carrying his broom.*) What's the matter, old-timer? Stage fright? Play for the people. Let's hear what you can do.

OLD MAN

(*whispers*) Why is there an audience? I was told the theatre was closed all this week.

SETH

Well, nobody told them, and you're all they've got to see, 'cept me and

ENCORE

Ben. So it's up to you. (*He lays down his broom.*) Here, let's move your seat down this way a bit. (*The old man stands and Seth drags the chair he was sitting on downstage.*) Right. Your public awaits, Maestro.

OLD MAN

I can't perform. I haven't prepared anything. (*He speaks throughout with gentle good humor.*)

SETH

Beggars can't be choosers. When people drop in unexpected, they get potluck. Now if you'll just get yourself comfortable, we can get started.

OLD MAN

Wait — this guitar has no strings.

SETH

That's an oversight if I ever saw one. What the hell are you doing with a useless thing like that?

OLD MAN

It's a prop. I picked it up while I was wandering around backstage. It felt good to hold it, and I was daydreaming, pretending to play. I used to give concerts on this very stage, many years ago. I could even hear the music before you turned on the lights. (*He hums a few notes.*)

SETH

Well, the show must go on. One way or the other we'll squeeze a concert out of you. Look, the best thing is for you to go on pretending. We'll play records and make out that it's you.

OLD MAN

I don't think it will fool anyone.

SETH

Try, Pops. Have faith in yourself. (*The old man tries to object, but Seth overrules him by ignoring him.*) Hey, Benny. Put on one of them old guitar records. Turn it up real loud.

BENNY

(*off*) Okay.

SETH

Look, Maestro. These people paid a lot of money, so make it good. Give them some of that fancy fandango stuff. But not too much, now. Never give a mob all they want. Just lead them on a bit. Make them think there's more where that came from. Know what I mean?

OLD MAN

I think so. After all, I was very well received in my day. On tour, I could command a full house with only twenty-four hours' advance notice.

SETH

That's nothing: you just got yourself an audience with no warning at all.

DAVID KORR

Hey, how do you turn this thing on?

SETH

(*peers off into the darkness*) Just up on your left. Yeah, those. That's it. (*The stage is bathed in intense yellow light.*) No, no. Up in the next row.

BENNY

Okay, that's got it. (*over the loudspeaker*) One guitar coming up. (*The yellow lights go off.*)

SETH

Ready? This is your big moment. You're about to make a comeback.

OLD MAN

I'll try. We certainly can't disappoint an audience, can we. It's nice being back up here. (*There is the sound of a needle being placed scratchily on a record.*)

SETH

Here we go. (*He raises his arms as if to conduct an orchestra. The music comes on loud and harsh. It is blue-grass banjo. The old man is poised, ready to "play." He lowers the guitar and looks beseechingly at Seth, who is conducting furiously. Seth stops when he sees that the old man isn't playing.*) Hey, you're supposed to be playing. What's the matter, Chief?

OLD MAN

(*barely audible over the music*) It's not a guitar.

SETH

Eh?

OLD MAN

It's not a guitar.

SETH

You sure? (*The old man nods. Seth listens.*) You're right. It's a goddamn mandolin or something like that. Won't work, huh?

OLD MAN

I'm afraid not.

SETH

Hey, Ben! Ben! Turn it off. (*There is a loud scratching and the music stops. Ben's voice comes over the loudspeaker.*)

BENNY

What's the matter?

SETH

Wrong stuff.

BENNY

You sure?

12

ENCORE

SETH

Yeah. The professor can't play that kind of music. It's got to be a proper guitar.

BENNY

Okay. Just a minute. Here's one. Some old guy with glasses.

SETH

Doesn't matter. Put it on. Ready, Maestro? Here we go again. (*This time it is a guitar: beautiful, complex, and melodic. The old man pretends to pluck and finger abstractedly, with no enthusiasm. Soon, however, he is caught up in the music and listens with deep and emotional appreciation. He forgets he is supposed to be miming. Seth notes this and watches him in extreme annoyance. He finally kicks the old man's foot.*) Hey, what's the matter now?

OLD MAN

Nothing. Glorious, isn't it?

SETH

Great. So play.

OLD MAN

I'm sorry. I couldn't. You see, it's not my music. Someone far greater than I is on that record. It would be sinful to pretend those miraculous sounds came from me. They have a delicacy and a precision these old fingers could never hope to mimic. I'm sorry.

SETH

The first one wasn't good enough and now this one's too good. Make up your mind. Listen, they don't know it's not you. For all they know it's the queen of Sheba. They don't even care, long as it sounds all right, and they're the ones who paid for it. So who're you to go all particular? Doesn't matter whether you like the music or not — there's people waiting for a show. Now play.

OLD MAN

It's very difficult. I'm not familiar with the piece.

SETH

Just move your fingers. Benny's doing all the work. (*The old man gives Seth a small, sad smile, and with a deep breath returns to his task. Seth stands back, watching intently to see that the old man doesn't slack off again, and conducts nonchalantly with one hand. Occasionally he turns and looks into the wings and nods to Benny. The old man has shut his eyes and lost himself in the music. He has really dreamed himself into a concert and is swept along by the sounds he is pretending to make. Seth has a sudden and apparently amusing thought, and he goes off to speak to Benny.*

DAVID KORR

At the end of the piece, the old man almost collapses over his guitar. He has genuinely worked, and is still entranced by the spell and his communion with the music. Suddenly, thunderous applause comes over the loudspeaker. The old man, still hypnotized, rises, holding the guitar in one hand, and steps forward and begins taking slow, deep bows — to the right, the center, and the left. He keeps his head down in humble gratitude and opens his arms wide in an expression of thanks. Seth creeps on to watch him in disbelief and growing amusement. Finally, he gives a cut sign to Benny, and the applause stops as suddenly as it began. The old man freezes and Seth casts a handful of plastic flowers at him.) Encore! Encore! Hooah ha ha. Oh ho. Benny, did you see that? Oh Jesus.

OLD MAN

(waits until Seth has finished laughing) You have fooled an old man. He was willing to perform a service so that these people needn't be turned away, and you played on his age and his silly daydreams to turn him into an exhibition. I suppose it's my own fault. I deserve it for being gullible. Is it so amusing?

SETH

It's not really you, Professor, though I will say you put on a fine show. It's the whole idea — one recording bowing to another. Oh dear, I'm near dead with laughing.

OLD MAN

One recording bowing to another. I see what you mean. *(He begins picking up the plastic flowers.)* It might well have been. With the lights in my eyes I can't see if it's those people out there applauding or not. And if we were clever, they might never know it was a recording *they* were hearing. It's all the same. *(He hands Seth the flowers. The guitar music comes back on over the speaker. He listens for a moment.)* Well, let's tidy up. Tomorrow's another day. *(He hands Seth the guitar, then retrieves the broom and starts carefully sweeping the downstage area.)*

SETH

Hey, wait a second. What are you doing?

OLD MAN

Just taking the opportunity to be useful. Sweeping.

SETH

I can see that. But you're wasting your time. I've already done that part.

OLD MAN

Are you sure? It's quite filthy.

SETH

'Course I'm sure. It doesn't matter, does it? They can't see it from out there.

14

ENCORE

OLD MAN

You're quite right. I needn't bother. Come along, then. I'll buy you a drink.

SETH

Now you're talking. (*He tosses the guitar on the heap of props.*) There's a good place around the corner.

OLD MAN

What about your friend?

SETH

He'll have to skip it tonight. He has to put the applause on when the music's finished.

BENNY

(*coming on stage*) No, I don't. I put it on the changer. It'll come on automatic.

SETH

Well, come on then. But go back and close the curtain first. (*Benny does so.*)

THE END

Encore by David Korr was presented August 15, 27, 29 and September 3, 19, 1970, at the Other Place Theatre, the experimental stage of The Guthrie Theater, Minneapolis. It was directed by Dan Bly.

Cast of Characters

BENNY	William Levis
SETH	Dan Bly
OLD MAN	Stephen Keep

15

GLADDEN SCHROCK

Madam Popov

A PLAY IN ONE ACT

Cast of Characters

MADAM POPOV, indefinite in age, vulgarity and grace combined
SPUD, squat, numb, peasantish
RORO, muscular, humorless; in another place and time might
be a construction foreman
DEETRUM, old, methodic, lean, butlerish
POSTMASTER, heavy but jolly, whitening at the temples

MADAM POPOV

A castle. A few deranged lights illuminate a dusty throne flanked by a weird assortment of chairs, stuffed animals, a trunk of threadworn but once fashionable clothes, a plow beam and various other instruments of labor. Stage right is relatively bare except for an old refectory table, above which dangles a knife. The knife is weighted at the hilt with a cast-iron ball and is held up by a rope which, by a series of pulleys and clews, attaches to a triplock at the neckrest of the throne. On the wall at stage left are simulated french windows. Through them it appears one can see the sun, vines, birds, and animals in a forest. These are all obviously *painted on the wall. This might well be achieved by the use of a scrim. Madam Popov enters. She is aging and somewhat dowdy in her old regalia. She has long, vaguely beautiful and distempered hair neither combed nor cared for. She moves to the french doors like someone taking the first deep breath of morning air.*

MADAM POPOV

Ah! Beautiful! Beautiful day. Beautiful annual Monday's Sunday. (*laughs girlishly*) Here birdie birdie. Hungry? Hungry, twit twit birdies? (*Takes a pan from the floor, goes to the trunk, rummages, lifts out several ears of corn, and shells them on an enormous old sheller of the wheel variety. She hums faintly the shepherd's tune of later in the play. She replaces the pan of corn on the floor.*) There, birdie birdie. Beautiful corn on a beautiful morn. Not hungry, eh? Never mind. Eat it when no one is here to frighten you. We haven't long to live. Not long. We haven't long. (*a foretaste of her final disgust*) Damned fool chirpers of the woods. (*She takes a huge and battered calendar from the trunk, sits with it upon the throne, trying to discover the date.*) This . . the thirty-second year of our Lord. Lessness.

19

(*laughs at her joke*) Infallible dates. Let's see. Shrove to Ash? No, past, past. Let's see. All Fool's? No. Past. Daily I think. (*laughs at her joke*) The moon . . sixth apogee, past, nearing its seventh. No. Hmmmmmmm. No. Hmmmmmmm. Here . . Here we are . . Here it is. The black circle. Oh, I felt it, I knew it in my bones. Dear Father, here it is. Thirty-third year of my atonement. Cacklaw Castle, we have arrived! (*She puts the calendar away, sits on the throne, looks off right impatiently. Rings a small desk bell. No answer. A cow bell. No answer. In a rage she clangs an enormous dinner bell. There is a patter of feet off right. The door flies open and two servants, Spud and Roro, dash in.*)

RORO

(*out of breath*) The Madam rang?

MADAM POPOV

Of course I rang, you walleyed idiots. The sun is up. Time to work.

RORO

Might I point out to the Madam that here at Cacklaw the sun is always up?

MADAM POPOV

Certainly not. You, Spud, your shirt is open. And for goodness' sake fasten your fly. (*Spud repairs his person.*) A nice couple of goose-headed servants you are.

RORO

May I suggest to the Madam, it's hardly possible —

MADAM POPOV

Oh, don't quibble, Roro. Don't pick nitties. You see me? Eh? I'm up early. In fact I haven't slept. Today is a rare bird finally caught, and we must set it free. I expect you to function at your pitch and not snarl around me like dry and feckless . . gemsboks.

RORO

(*not trusting his ears*) Gemsboks, Madam?

MADAM POPOV

Gemsboks, exactly.

SPUD

(*his mirth scarcely repressed*) Gemsboks!

MADAM POPOV

Gemsboks, gemsboks! Beasties of the Moor.

RORO

(*always the diplomat*) Dry and feckless gemsboks, yes, Madam. The Madam has the assurance of our best services.

MADAM POPOV

(*more pleasantly*) Well now I didn't mean to scold my boys. Here, Roro, come sit. And you, Spud, with your droopy peasant ears and mushmeal eyes. (*They sit uneasily at the foot of the throne.*) We've been together a long time, haven't we, doing our business lo these years? You're decent enough fellows, if you are rather numb. But I think you understand the meaning of Cacklaw Castle.

RORO

(*quickly, a tired recitative*) The world's no plaything and life's no joy.

SPUD

Forever and amen.

MADAM POPOV

Bravo. And do you know what day this is? Spud, you tell me. Quick now.

SPUD

Uh . . Monday. (*Roro hits him on the head. Spud topples over, scrambles up again.*)

RORO

It is Sunday, birthday of Cacklaw Castle.

SPUD

But no . . I think . . I thought yesterday — (*Roro hits him again. Same business.*)

MADAM POPOV

Yesterday was Sunday by chance. Today it is Sunday by necessity. (*pointedly*) We make the world, Spud, we make the world.

SPUD

(*eagerly reciting*) For man fitteth as a bind blird, and plight . . er . . and lath . . uh . .

RORO

(*covering*) Man flitteth as a blind bird until the path is hewn and light has shown his way. (*He raises his hand to strike Spud again, thinks better of it. Spud nonetheless falls and scrambles up.*)

MADAM POPOV

We may flatter ourselves that we have found a great light. A beacon.

RORO

(*still thinking there is reasonableness abroad*) Pardon, Madam, but of what use is light —

MADAM POPOV

An example shining for our race.

RORO

Might I bother to suggest —

MADAM POPOV

We've kept aloof from the world's trivia.

RORO

Please allow me the impertinence, Madam, to advise that in the world outside, having never been there, never being seen there . . it's sometimes difficult . . that is, to be effective a beacon must —

MADAM POPOV

Oh don't be an ass. What do I care for the "world outside"? For the sniveling marketgoers, the gooey-snouted merchants and middlemen passing their time in ignorance? What do I care for mongers of every sort on all sides of us, whoring their wares? Oh I know them, know 'em down to their last scratch and gaggle. They have a pig's mind for pleasure and a calf's bawl finally for their tragedy. But one by one they'll learn what we . . what *I* have learned already — the blessed balm of seclusion. Now hop to it. You've not forgotten your duties?

RORO

No, Madam. I pull the curtains, clean the table, speak my piece.

MADAM POPOV

Good. (*She goes to examine the trunk. Spud and Roro stay behind.*)

SPUD

I serve the wine, recite the mother, and empty the corn so Madam thinks her painted birds have really — (*He is stopped short by Roro who pulls Spud's shirt over his head, clogging his mouth.*)

MADAM POPOV

(*indicating the trunk*) Your clothes are here. Shake the dust. (*points to the portals behind and above the throne*) And oil the curtain rods; they squeaked up last year's ceremony something fierce. (*finally back to them, face to face*) And please try, TRY not to be such lagging . .

RORO

Gemsboks, yes, Madam.

MADAM POPOV

Imbeciles was the word. (*She exits. Roro slaps his sides in supreme disgust.*)

RORO

(*in lieu of bigger things to attack*) Why can't you shut it up when she's excited?

SPUD

Please don't be angry, Roro.

RORO

Why can't you? I have to lug you around like a boil. Coddle and take care . .

SPUD

I'll oil all the curtains myself. I'll dust. (*on his knees*) I'll let you beat me with a rope. (*Pause. Sings.*) "Happy birthday, Dear Cacklaw . ." (*weeps*)

22

MADAM POPOV

RORO

Oh for God's sake, don't wet yourself. Don't mess up your gullet.

SPUD

But I'm unhappy. What I see around me is only what I don't see, you see. And what I don't see makes me afraid. It's fear that causes me to bumble.

RORO

(*pats the poor fellow's shoulder*) Oh well. We have to stick together. Have to keep together somehow, if we're to survive.

SPUD

I try hard. Don't be furious. Try so hard.

RORO

(*big brother*) Aha! But the rewards aren't for trying. They are for . . KNOWING! (*Sits beside Spud on the floor. Grandiloquently at the start, petering soon into nonsense, he commences.*) Life . . is simply a huge . . marble . . falling . . sifting down through . . melted . . inkstands. (*He is visibly none too happy with where his ad-lib homily led him.*)

MADAM POPOV'S VOICE

(*from off, shrieking*) The sun is too high! It's the last year! It must set! Listen to me!

DEETRUM'S VOICE

(*from off, throughout her screeching*) But Madam . . Yes, Madam . . But, however, Madam . . (*With a boom and a blast the Madam bursts through the door, dragging Deetrum by the ear, and deposits him on the floor. Spud and Roro cower in the corner.*)

MADAM POPOV

What a household! Not a one of you slag-heaped gabbling rodents knows your place!

DEETRUM

But, Madam, never . . ! That is, to my knowledge, never have we fully . . uh . . set the sun.

MADAM POPOV

Get the paints! Survey it! I've fed you these many years and my father fed before me, and for what? To hear your wheezing chicken voices stammering about the sun not setting at the end of things? TODAY IT SETS! (*Spots Spud and Roro. Drives them backwards across the room.*) And you two lamepated shitepolks standing there, what are you doing? Prepare for the service. Make it smooth. Move, march, run! (*Having reached her extremity, Madam Popov wipes her forehead, sits down, breathes deeply, relaxes, cools, and even laughs at herself a little eventually as she adjusts her frontage*

23

apparel.) Whew! There now. If I'm not careful I'll have my girlie business bouncing around here every which way. It's the excitement does it, you understand. Has me . . upended. Whew, there now. (*composed*) Deetrum, you scour the city for the sacrifice. You can do that much without protest, can't you?

DEETRUM

Yes, Madam.

RORO

But it's *my* year . . *my* year to get the sacrifice.

MADAM POPOV

No. I don't want another drunken rumbunny from the pub.

RORO

But, Madam, if they're not drunk they'll tattle on us and be believed.

MADAM POPOV

There'll be no tattling, I assure you. Well, are you paralyzed? Huzzah! Busy! Work! Work! (*As they chant the following, done as a "round," they set about hurriedly tidying the room. They rush in circles, generally to little avail, if any avail at all, often undoing what the others have done. But they give the impression of great industry, which after all is what work is all about.*)

ALL THREE

Work, work, work, work,
Use the fingers, use the feet,
Slave until the castle's neat.
WORK, work, work, work,
Wash the tapestries, the floor,
Flit the dirties from the door.
Scrub immaculately clean,
Dirt is cousin to obscene.
Work, work, work, work.

MADAM POPOV

(*applauding them*) That's better. Bravo. Now finish for the service. (*She exits. All sit on the floor.*)

DEETRUM

I am tired to death.

RORO

(*after a pause*) Life's ways have grown impossible. We can't go on.

DEETRUM

Life's ways . . (*somewhat in Roro's manner above, evidently a favorite pastime around the castle*) Life . . is a small . . sifting . . falling . . caravan.

24

RORO

(*showing his shoe*) See this? Look here. My lash is untied. Did it on purpose. I arose this morning, dusted my room, glared in the mirror and said to myself, ''Roro, you are an individual. You have innate distinction. Leave your lash untied.''

DEETRUM

Courageous, man.

SPUD

Bold.

RORO

It's necessary. (*thinking*) Cacklaw is murdering our finer qualities. (*pause*) Let's think something. (*pause*) Let's plan something. (*pause*) Let's do something. (*Long pause. Dawning on him.*) Let's revolt!

SPUD

(*aghast*) Revolt?

RORO

Why not? Revolt and be done with it.

DEETRUM

Revolt, eh? What a curious thought. Well, I'll drink to the spirit of that anyhow, yes indeed.

SPUD

Is there wine left?

RORO

Always wine, always wine. (*starts off after it*)

SPUD

But do we dare?

RORO

(*wheeling around*) Dare? Why not? Are we so flea-peed and cowardly? Look here, I'm free. I do what I like. (*lies down on the floor, face down*)

DEETRUM

Me too. Unshackled. At the snap of a hat. (*makes what once would have been a neat leap onto the throne*)

RORO

Life is to get what we can of it. (*pounds the floor*)

DEETRUM

Free men fear nothing. (*Swings his feet over the back of the throne. His back is on the seat and his head dangles in the front, upside down and toward the audience.*)

RORO

Free men make their own compass. (*rolls about on the floor*)

25

DEETRUM

Free men indulge their talents. (*somersaults backwards off the throne, landing on his feet, somewhat amazed at himself*)

RORO

Freedom! (*Boro leaps about the room like a frog. Spud, who has been watching with increasing excitement, finally lets out an exuberant yell, lifts the plow beam above his head, and thunders it across the room, nearly shattering the trunk in the bargain. As if that were not enough, he then turns in tight circles, his arms flapping, screeching "freedom" all the while. Deetrum and Roro, scared white, tackle him and drag him behind the throne, from which protective warren they then peer tremulously toward the door. Quavering*) What in the hell do you go banging around like a bullock for? You'll get us fired, moron. (*Spud begins to whimper.*)

DEETRUM

(*hits Spud*) SHHHHHHHH! (*pause*) Think she heard?

RORO

(*hits Deetrum*) SHHHHHHHHHHHHHHHHHHHH!! (*sound of a door slamming*) She's coming!

DEETRUM

We're in for it now. I'm going to tell. He needs a good thrashing, that's what. (*Spud whimpers again. Roro puts his hand over Spud's mouth. Another door slam.*)

RORO

There. She's gone out.

DEETRUM

Out? She never goes out.

RORO

Then she went to the vaults.

SPUD

The vaults!

RORO

Yes. She's gone to the vaults.

SPUD

But . . she'll see they're empty!

DEETRUM

In thirty-two years she's never noticed.

RORO

Of course she's noticed. She knows it. She's never killed a man in her life.

MADAM POPOV

DEETRUM

On the contrary. I say she thinks she's murdered the lot of them. Thirty-two vaults, thirty-two dead men.

RORO

SHHHHHHHHHHHHH!! (*They listen. No sound.*) That was close. (*gets up*) Next time, you fly-blown mule, don't stir things up. (*replaces the plow beam*)

DEETRUM

I'd better set the sun. (*He goes to the trunk, brings out surveyor's equipment.*)

SPUD

I'm wondering . .

DEETRUM

Now what?

SPUD

About the wine.

DEETRUM

Wine, yes. Fetch it. Help me, eh, Roro? I've forgotten how. We never set it before. Something's in the air.

RORO

You survey. I wipe. Then I mark. Then you paint. Simple as that. (*As Deetrum finishes setting up, Spud takes a cloth out of his pocket, goes to the throne, lifts the seat, removes a bottle of wine and glasses. He fills the glasses, looks at Deetrum and Roro, downs one glassful, fills again, gives each a glass. Roro, tasting, speaks.*) Good. Despite the vinegars. (*Pause. Looks at Spud.*) Mental function. (*pause*) Fa-ci-li-tate.

DEETRUM

(*muttering to himself*) Six and three minutes . . (*looking into apparatus*) recorded briefly nineteen-six. Good wine. Decrease twenty minutes per year. Angle at one degree nine. Excellent wine. (*glasses refilled all around*) Sun at dark minus angular diffusion. Red light long rays. Bold painting. Hold the marker. (*Roro does so at the painting.*) Over. Right. Up. Too far. Down. That's it. Further. Down. Ah! Down. Ah! Further . . AAAAAAHH. Fuuuuuuurtherr! Furrrrrrrrrrrrrrtherrrrrrrrr! AAAAAAAAAAAAAAAAAAAAH! There. Hold. Mark. (*Roro marks. Deetrum slips a tin of water paints from his pocket, runs to the painted doors, begins to paint in evening colors a new sun almost completely set. Roro puts away the surveyor's equipment.*) Round strokes. Bold strokes. Blaze the forest. (*steps on the plate of corn*) Dammit. Take the pan, Spud, I've made a mess.

SPUD

But the birds don't eat till four o'clock.

DEETRUM

It's past four. The sun's down. Take the pan.

SPUD

I mean the real four, the outside four. She'd object.

DEETRUM

To hell with her! Oooooh, the wine's up there already. Today it doesn't matter when the birds feed.

SPUD

But Madam —

RORO

Take the goddamned thing away. Her painted birds don't eat and she knows it. (*Spud lifts the broken trunk lid, empties the corn beneath some old garments. Roro lifts his glass with significance.*) Here's to wine, the wench of freedoms. (*The other two lift their glasses also, slightly tipsy already, mumbling the oath, and then return to their work.*)

SPUD

(*sitting in the middle of the floor*) I remember once I went down to the city pond. No, really, I've been outside the castle. Though I hardly remember it. When I was a child. Childlike. There were swans and fish and . . water roaches. An old man wept for not having crumbs enough to feed the living things.

RORO

(*tuning up, expansively*) You remember, Deetrum, when we were boys? Unwinding the village clocks. Huh? Smearing the backside of the mayor's statue, sometimes daily? Ah, those years. You were going to be a painter, and I a potter. Or was it the other way?

DEETRUM

We had our moments. And women!

RORO

Falling about us. Not a spot in the hay got cold one night to the next.

DEETRUM

Two-hour chase, four hours down.

RORO

Two and three a night.

DEETRUM

(*putting down his paints*) Remember old Longlegs? Ran like a deer. Said she wouldn't, would never, never would . . But she did! And no coin on the loggerhead.

RORO

(*grandly*) I was a titan once. Nothing could stir my hackles. I'd waken in the darkest shadows, when the moon was full and the rising tide brought anger to every shore; and I'd dash out into the midnight mists, half-naked, plundering my way through the pitch; and I'd steal the widow's horn, and blow it long and oh so proudly from the golden-rimmed hill above Stover's shithouse. (*Roro leaps up onto the throne.*) Tahoot, Tahoot . . TAHOOOOOOOOOOOOOOOOOOTTEEEEEEEEEEEEEEEE!! Oh, they'd threaten me of course. Sic their bur-hounds on my heels and flounce against my withers. They'd fire their guns! But I'd blast my wild tahoooooties all the louder. TAHOOOOOOOOOOOTTEEEEEEEEEEEEEE!! (*meditatively, a bit moved*) It's great at least once to have felt that spirit in the breech. To be master. King! (*In conclusion he makes a magnificent gesture. His hand alas falls heavily enough upon the neckrest to trigger the lethal business. The knife whistles with a shrill of death into the table. They are terrified: All scramble for cover. Presently Roro revives, albeit still shaken and shaking. With simplicity*) See what globs of cowering dung we have become? Give me the rope. We'll latch it again, simple as that. (*Spud gives Roro the rope. Deetrum pulls the knife from the table with some difficulty, and Roro fastens it again. Roro continues his peroration with diminished magnificence.*) We were all titans once. But now look. Defeated. Broken. Sad simpering servants, every one of us. Shattered. "Clean the floors," and we clean. "Feed the birdies. Paint the sun. Kill some poor son of a bitch off the street." And we do it; oh we do it all neatly, to the very last pin and pinhole of obedience. (*walks to the painted doors*) Look at it. Pigment on a wall.

DEETRUM

Of course it is. Brushwork on paper.

RORO

Is it real? No! Birds are where birds are. Trees stand only where trees only stand.

DEETRUM

The sun is nowhere but in the sky, where the sun is.

RORO

But *we* know what's up. (*stamps foot*) There. That's real. I can feel it. The boards creak. I can hear it. (*stamps again*) Friends, that's a fact of which we can be certain.

DEETRUM

(*clapping his hands*) I'm doing a true thing over here.

RORO

Gentlemen, were we to pool our various brains and sundry grievances, we could start a new life, a new style. A cult of actual freedoms!

DEETRUM

(*considering*) We're old.

RORO

Old, yes. But hang it all we're not so slacked-backed and jelly-bellied we couldn't take the castle over and make real the real that's really real.

DEETRUM

Revolt? You mean . . not just in idle thought . . nor playroom skirmish . . but actually — ?

RORO

The whole hog, lips, tits, and tailhole. If Cacklaw were ours — ! (*A door slams, resounding throughout the castle. Immediate bedlam, everyone rushing about, chanting the "Work Round." The glasses and paints are put away. Roro takes a can of oil from the trunk, scampers through a curtained opening behind the wall above the throne, where two picture frames are cut through, covered by traverse curtains. He oils the rods and motions Spud to try the draw . . which works after a moment of difficulty. Deetrum is dusting the room with what appears to be his handkerchief, when the Madam enters buoyantly.*)

MADAM POPOV

Ah, quivers . . rumbles . . tremors of excitement in the house! The verge of some great revolution, I feel it.

RORO

(*shaken*) Revolution, Madam?

MADAM POPOV

(*lyrically*) Today is a sonnet whose trailing couplet will be the blood union of two hearts that rhyme, or did once. (*Spud stands utterly confounded.*) Dear Spud, you don't understand? You shall, soon enough. It burns in my veins like a vintaged wine.

SPUD

(*there's a word he understands*) Wine? Uh, no wine at all, Madam.

RORO

We're ready, Madam.

MADAM POPOV

Good. I'm eager to get on.

DEETRUM

The sun, Madam. Scarcely visible.

MADAM POPOV

Excellent.

SPUD

I've oiled the curtains.

RORO

I oiled the curtains.

30

MADAM POPOV

SPUD

(*weakly*) He oiled the curtains.

MADAM POPOV

And I've been to the vaults. They are well limed. The caskets are rusty, but that's to be expected. There are but two empty remaining. We've filled thirty-two in as many years.

SPUD

(*to Deetrum*) Psst! Isn't true.

DEETRUM

(*covering*) I take it then, Madam, we have one year to go?

MADAM POPOV

(*pause; quietly*) We shall see, we shall see. Put your things on. (*Spud and Roro go to the trunk and begin dressing in costume. Spud wears the clothes of an old woman. Roro assumes the gallant if tattered and shrunken attire of an aging gentleman of the Old World. An enormous black hat.*) Deetrum . . (*Deetrum steps forward.*) It's up to you to bring our . . guest. I have checked all possible information and conclude the Postmaster is our man. Make no mistake. You'll find him at his work. An industrious soul with large hands and a shock of brown hair, tinged now with white, I'd guess. Oh, I'm champing to get on with it.

SPUD

(*to Roro*) The Postmaster! We'll get a drubbing from the town this time, you wait.

MADAM POPOV

Bring him in at the correct moment.

DEETRUM

Yes, Madam. (*He exits. Madam Popov sits on the throne.*)

MADAM POPOV

You remember the words?

RORO

Of course, Madam.

MADAM POPOV

Let us begin. (*Spud and Roro exit behind the throne. They soon appear at the picture frames as portraits. The Madam leans back as if in profound meditation. Presently she lifts her head, transformed. Rises slowly, face radiant. Walks about the room touching things, uttering cries of delight suitable to a young girl. Strokes the plow beam.*) Form. Graceful. Worn grain. History of the earth. Proud furrow through marsh and hummock. Memories.

RORO

(*posing*) Your heritage, daughter.

31

GLADDEN SCHROCK

MADAM POPOV

Father! You're home! (*turns slightly, does not look at the portrait*)

RORO

Keep it, daughter. It is yours. A monument to honest labor.

SPUD

(*posing*) Keever! You're home.

RORO

I've come the long and tortuous way, my dear. The horse is tired.

SPUD

It's been longer than a year, I've counted the days. But I knew, Keever. When I awoke this morning, I knew. For the air was still, the birds sang, and the sun had already whisked the screw off from the . . uh . . well —

RORO

(*to Spud, a hiss*) Kissed the dew from off the hills, you bug-assed cretin.

SPUD

(*to Roro*) I never get that —

RORO

The words, the words!

SPUD

. . And I knew! Today my husband would come home.

RORO

Ceaselessly I thanked God for the wife and child. Come, daughter; kiss me. (*pantomine of a kiss, both looking front*)

SPUD

We have kept our pledge.

RORO

Daughter? Have you been true?

MADAM POPOV

Not once, not for a heartbeat, have I strayed.

RORO

That's music for a tired man.

MADAM POPOV

Tell me of your journey. (*sits at the foot of the throne, leaning back as if against his knee*)

RORO

The world is still there, my child.

MADAM POPOV

And green? With ivy and trilliums? Eglantine and roses? Honeysuckle and . . vetch?

MADAM POPOV

RORO

Still there and lush and elegantly flowered. I slept deep in its bosom, where the morning brings us all that had been lost.

SPUD

(*vehemently*) Oh, I know; she plied you with her fat breasts, you balding devil!

RORO

(*to Spud*) Later! We're not there! (*Spud indicates it's all too much for him. Roro goes on.*) I walked for days across the moor, eating herbs, drinking from rivulets parting meadows. And when the road went rough, I labored thews and sinews for a smith, till I could buy his horse and carry on.

SPUD

But tell her of people. Our daughter matures; she has a woman's body now.

RORO

(*unheeding*) The pure trees . . virginal, unviolated.

SPUD

(*washerwoman*) Tell her of people and their loves.

RORO

Yes. People. A dismal tale. I must pause. (*He does. Ten seconds. Spud gets nervous.*)

SPUD

Am I on? (*Roro, himself too nervous about remembering upcoming words to tolerate Spud's goofs and capers, disappears from his portal. Shortly thereafter Spud lunges forward with remarkable vigor, gasps, and nearly falls. Roro reappears presently at his own frame and they continue. Madam meanwhile, in her entrancement, has not noticed.*)

RORO

I reflect on people. I am sure that in the beginning God had a plan . . one of unfolding beauties. And man was to crown it all, germ to the fallow midden. Well, the corpse of it came well enough; the Firmament was the body, the fingers the Milky Way, and the several suns lay pitted in its eyes. But when Man the Soul came, supposing to give it blood and spirit and whatever, he came instead like a vague green viscous liquid, bubbling with putrid faith and ordured ego, and the corpse has sorrowed since from that indulgence worse even than was its beginning. Oh I've seen it. Beneath the oak copse on Dole Mountain I found maidens yawning their hunks at two pence a poke. Strange-looking kidloids milled about the grounds, raucous with wine and brutal instruments, singing in their sweaty youthful tempest. Sin came! And man's sin is always that he celebrates the kingdom as it is, instead of forcing it, molding it to order!

33

MADAM POPOV

But I've been true, Father. I've walked the mornings like a white and listless kitten. Evenings I have peered alone, watching life's enormous stillness shunt from star to star. And I knew, Father, I knew that it was good.

RORO

(*definitive*) But man is not! (*pause*) How old are you?

MADAM POPOV

Twenty-five.

RORO

A babe; a mere child.

SPUD

Oh come on. She's no pimpled toddler on the pap, if that's what you mean.

RORO

She has much to learn. Life has how many ways a leaf can drift in a wind.

SPUD

(*utterly scornful*) And death is a plucked pheasant gagging its brains in the bushes.

RORO

(*intimately*) Listen, for I am getting old: Life is to be controlled as numbers are to be counted. A fallen tree does not make the ax, nor does sunrise turn the earth.

MADAM POPOV

Oh I love you for that, Father.

SPUD

Bilge-blow!

RORO

And I you, daughter. Yet . . someday . . you'll want another man, a stranger.

MADAM POPOV

Oh, there is someone already. Just a lad. A shepherd. I hear him each dawn gathering his sheep, passing the castle, and the song he sings going with them to the mountains. (*sings*)

> Little sheep, frightened lamb,
> Mist is off the buttercup,
> The sun is up.
> Little friend, woolly friend,
> Today I'll play my flute for you.
> I've never had a kiss and so
> I'll play it low.

He has brown hair, long and graceful, a beautiful shock. Hasn't seen me,

34

but I hum his tune when he passes and he knows I'm here; for he looked up once and laughed . . but I hid from him.

SPUD

Love is wonderful.

RORO

Balderbeans! It's deceptive. A woman's brains are between her legs.

SPUD

Don't yell at daughter, she has her rights.

RORO

You ignoramus. You haven't so much as crossed the road and still you order me about as if I were invalid.

SPUD

How could I travel, you pus-gutted puritan, when you lock me up here like a tinker's toy?

MADAM POPOV

Father, I've never seen a full day out-of-doors from shadow to shadow. Never water nor the wings of birds not scrawled on paper.

RORO

But I've described it to you, haven't I? Glowering bowels, isn't that enough? Oh I see it, the two of you at home, conniving for your freedom, while I've been out seeking substance.

SPUD

Substance! You don't fool me, you sweaty-legged coot. You've been out after pleasure. Deny it! You've been to the inn by the lake where that slimy bitch Freida tends bar.

RORO

Yes . . if it's any of your concern. One probes the wound to find its cure.

SPUD

And she plied you with her fat breasts, you balding devil! (*looks triumphantly at Roro for having got it right*)

RORO

It is my cross to be misunderstood. Not I alone walked the earth's crust; you and daughter went proxy with me. It was for you.

SPUD

Blueballs and bullrot.

MADAM POPOV

I believe you, Father. But my breasts are large now, my voice is strong. I too want to love.

RORO

(*dejected*) Very well, then. Go at it.

35

MADAM POPOV

Judge me. This is how I would do it. (*She walks to the door as if greeting someone.*) I go to where the shepherd lives. I take his hand. (*Waits. Door does not open.*) I go to where the shepherd lives. I take his . . Deetrum! (*suddenly awful*) DEEEEEEEETRUUUUUUUUUM!! You maundering shitbeetle, get in here!! (*Footsteps. The door bursts open. Deetrum stands trembling.*) You've messed it up.

DEETRUM

I have the Postmaster, Madam.

MADAM POPOV

Not yet! The part, the part. Play your part. (*resumes intimate girl quality immediately*) I go to where the shepherd lives; I take his hand. (*takes Deetrum's hand*) I'd stroll with him into the actual woods. (*Deetrum hums the tune of the shepherd's song. Madam leads him to the painting.*)

RORO

Look at her feeling him up with her eyes.

MADAM POPOV

My name is Vera.

DEETRUM

Hello, Vera. I'm Hans.

MADAM POPOV

Aren't these woods . . glorious?

RORO

Tripe.

SPUD

Keever.

DEETRUM

Yes, everything holds a secret here. The linnets, the logs . . the leeches.

MADAM POPOV

I love you for that, Hans.

RORO

By God I'll stop it!

MADAM POPOV

Have you ever been kissed?

DEETRUM

Never.

MADAM POPOV

We may as well. We're to be married.

RORO

Married? Roaring ditchwater!

MADAM POPOV

SPUD

It's beautiful!

RORO

I'll show her what stuff I'm made of. I'll — (*The Madam suddenly draws Deetrum in for a long and heartless kiss. He was not prepared, and both of them sprawl to the floor. Madam, however, does not break character. Roro, on the other hand, in disbelief drops both jaw and character.*) Thundering clappers, Spud! Do you see that?

SPUD

She's really kissing!

RORO

Something's up this year, that's for sure . . Well, let's get to our lines. Let's go on. (*The kissing stops. Deetrum is amazed and somewhat smothered. Roro resumes character.*) A cheap and tawdry performance. She's as incompetent as all the rest.

SPUD

Incompetent? When I married you you couldn't zip after a flush without snagging your teapot.

MADAM POPOV

Hans, I want to have your child.

RORO

Jumping hell, Daughter, you come back here!

MADAM POPOV

No, Father, I love him. I'm leaving the castle.

DEETRUM

Please don't fight. If there's been a mistake —

RORO

Twenty-four years I've spent telling you what's real and what's not. Well, I'm done. I'm leaving. This time for good.

SPUD

You're finished anyhow, you sodden pissamire.

MADAM POPOV

No, Father, don't leave. Forgive me!

RORO

Too late, infant. Piddle your diddle somewhere else.

DEETRUM

(*comes to Madam Popov, puts his arms formally about her, and sticks his chin at Roro*) How dare you speak like that to her. A marvelous girl. I'll return to this castle and take her away. (*For which resolution she slaps him abruptly along his ear, surprising Deetrum who was expecting the usual symbolic tap. It sends him rolling to the floor where he gladly remains until the close of this unhappy ceremony.*)

MADAM POPOV

Da-da . . !

RORO

A different tune now, isn't it. But it won't help. Go cover the earth on your own. See what squalid truths *you* stumble upon. Come, woman, we're done with her. (*with finality, back toward Madam*) Curses to the day you were conceived . . and on the pear tree where it happened. (*Roro and Spud disappear from their portals.*)

MADAM POPOV

(*inside herself*) I'll repent. I'll hide my shanks in Cacklaw all my life, and dream of unsoiled years before the fall, before the change. (*Now the histrionics come.*) I'll murder everything that tempts me otherwise. Oh as it was, dear Father, as it was. I loved it as it was! (*She collapses, rather too gracefully. Spud and Roro enter in due time from behind the throne, mopping their brows.*)

RORO

(*takes everything in, makes summation*) I'm getting too old for this. (*They begin to take off their things, stuffing them back into the trunk.*)

SPUD

Did you see it? She really kissed him.

RORO

Cacklaw can go to hell for all of me. I'm leaving. (*Spud grabs him, afraid; looks at Madam Popov who still weeps on the floor. Roro walks over to Deetrum, kicks him a couple of times.*)

DEETRUM

Huh? Oh. Oh my. Well! It was surely something this time around, wasn't it. (*gets to his feet, feels his face*) She plugged me a good one, no joke. (*Madam Popov makes a noise as if coming out of it.*)

RORO

Better get the guest. (*Deetrum and Roro exit. Spud looks about the room, goes to Madam. She has become quiet. He helps her up.*)

MADAM POPOV

(*simply*) A nice ceremony this year, Spud, don't you think?

SPUD

Very nice, Madam.

MADAM POPOV

How do I look?

SPUD

Madam looks fine.

MADAM POPOV

MADAM POPOV

Have the man brought in.

SPUD

Yes, Madam. (*He exits. The Madam goes to the trunk, takes out a white flowing shawl, and puts it on. Turns to gaze at the door, waiting. Presently Deetrum enters, bringing the Postmaster. His laughter is somewhat nervous, but all in all bountiful and round and to his credit. Madam and the Postmaster stare at one another for a long moment.*)

MADAM POPOV

(*pointedly enigmatic*) Good evening, Postmaster.

POSTMASTER

Uh, well yes, a beautiful evening. An excellent . . day.

MADAM POPOV

(*she gestures for Deetrum to seat him; the Postmaster is alarmed at everything and eyes Deetrum's movements suspiciously*) Please be seated. (*Deetrum, upon seating the Postmaster successfully, exits. Pause. Madam stares cool-ly at the Postmaster. He laughs nervously. She hisses a little, like a cat. He jumps. She smiles warmly. He fidgets. Attempts a smile.*) You're nervous, Postmaster. I'm sorry.

POSTMASTER

Uh, why yes . . I suppose I would be. I mean it's all a bit strange . . There I was, sitting peacefully at my work — nearly asleep I'll admit — when in popped your servant there, unannounced . . and he, he, why he just —

MADAM POPOV

Urged you to come with him.

POSTMASTER

Yes.

MADAM POPOV

(*kindly*) I hope he wasn't rude. (*As intended, her humane tone relaxes him. Clearly she's in control. Spud enters with a tray.*) Wine, Postmaster?

POSTMASTER

(*anything but*) Oh, delighted, delighted! Veritas en vino, et cetera . . ha ha ha! Er, that is, perhaps the truth of this bizarre . . (*Spud pours, exits.*) Yes . . it's been a wonderful day . . considering.

MADAM POPOV

(*lifts her glass*) To your health, sir.

POSTMASTER

(*eyeing the glass with more than indifferent doubt*) And yours, I'm sure.

MADAM POPOV

To your good memory.

POSTMASTER

And yours, yours too; ditto. (*She notes his hesitation; makes a point of drinking. He laughs, stops, laughs, stops, drops his glass to the floor.*) Oh I'm . . it's terribly . . most clumsy.

MADAM POPOV

(*takes his chin forcefully in her hand, a strong but ambiguous gesture*) Don't be afraid, sir. It will all be explained in due course. It'll be to our advantage to become quite frank with one another.

POSTMASTER

(*still wondering about the wine*) It's been so . . frank, yes . . so unusual finding people here at the castle . . supposedly vomited these many years.

MADAM POPOV

Vomited, sir?

POSTMASTER

Dear me, did I say vomited? Vacated. Vacated was my intention.

MADAM POPOV

The castle is by no means empty.

POSTMASTER

But how . . considering proximities and all that . . have you escaped being seen in the village?

MADAM POPOV

For thirty years I've not set foot outside these walls.

POSTMASTER

(*incredulous, his interest beginning to overtake his apprehension*) Well! That's something of a . . local phenomenon, now isn't it. Ha ha ha!

MADAM POPOV

(*knowing she's succeeded on one level, moves ahead, cutting into his laughter*) Are you married?

POSTMASTER

(*his words twisting around*) Oh yes . . very much . . I am. Married. (*She studies him. He continues out of sheer embarrassment.*) A bit late. Nine years now. You can see I'm graying; touch of sugar to sweeten our decline, ho ho. Three children. Two boys. Rather smart tykes if I do say so. Though the oldest is somewhat . . sputumish. Spits a lot. Keeps you busy with the mop. A usual family, I suppose, but then that's no discredit, is it?

MADAM POPOV

(*keeping him off balance*) Do you love your wife?

POSTMASTER

Well, now . . Yes I do. Why do you . . Yes, I'd say so.

MADAM POPOV

You have beautiful hair.

MADAM POPOV

POSTMASTER

Thank you. Not so handsome as it once was. It was then long, a great shock —

MADAM POPOV

Shock of brown, falling to the shoulders.

POSTMASTER

Yes! Indeed it was. That's . . amazing. I cut it for professional reasons when I became . . Most amazing.

MADAM POPOV

Are you aware, sir, how we sometimes make impressions, quite by accident, that affect others? Affect them deeply? Though not intentionally, perhaps. How we can upset or delay . . even destroy — simply by being seen at happenstance? Simply that.

POSTMASTER

(*as with most obsequious persons, he delights in any occasion to share confidences*) Yes . . well I suppose that's true. Yes, now that I think of it. And in all innocence. Take our office boy for example; rather a nitwit he was. Flitted about our counters like one of those scurvy chaps who hang always to the left of things. Although I admit he did his work. Common enough fellow . . Peter down the pike, you might say. But I did notice, however, how he watched me, hid behind my door sometimes, spied on me in conference. When the truth finally came out . . he thought I was a thief! (*laughs heartily*) Yes! Yes, it's a fact! There is a box, you see, in my desk, in which I keep rare stamps, fine stamps. He saw me checking it over once during the meal recess and construed it to mean I'd been snatching things: watches, chains, clockweights, I suppose, and hiding them. It swelled in his mind until he'd made quite a solid case out of it. (*pause*) Of course the police worked it out to everyone's satisfaction. (*pause*) That's . . quite true, yes, what you said.

MADAM POPOV

Then you'll understand why the boy *had* to defend his . . image of you, and go to the police. Right or wrong, such an impression is the basis of one's . . equilibrium; one's sense of what is actual. We've no choice but to build our lives on those chance cornerstones of impressions.

POSTMASTER

I daresay that's reasonable, yes.

MADAM POPOV

Then it follows, we are to be judged by the impressions we make.

POSTMASTER

In a way, yes. I see what you mean.

GLADDEN SCHROCK

MADAM POPOV

(*closing in*) So indeed you were culpable for that young man's apprehension. And paid for it in coin of inconvenience suffered at the police quarters.

POSTMASTER

Yes! My goodness, that roils up the soup a bit, doesn't it.

MADAM POPOV

(*with point*) You were fortunate, sir, it was no more serious. (*She walks about the room, dazzling him with pros and cons, which ripple out of her with ease.*) Is the man himself? Or is he but an image in other minds? Are we both ourselves and not ourselves; or different selves to each soul we inspire, each self thus bartered with impunity? And yet it's all us also, and we must answer for it all. Our impressions therefore . . our shadows, so to speak, in reality make fatter substance than do our solitary selves.

POSTMASTER

Mercy. That's a striking thought. If I catch the cut of it. (*He laughs, tugging at his knuckles.*)

MADAM POPOV

(*directly*) Are you happy?

POSTMASTER

Happy? Oh! Oh well now, I believe so. Yes, I can say it quite definitely. I love my work . . that's fortunate. Mornings, I stamp mail. Letters from here, yonder, wherever. Speedpost, special carrier. Each bearing a message. Birth, love, hope . . wars, debts, death. (*He'd not meant to ground out on such depressing shoals. Makes another go at it.*) At home I have my meals . . wife . . my children. Time passes. (*pause*) Well, a man learns what to expect. We live, and we die. We . . cannot alter the world. (*His laughter is now scarcely audible.*)

MADAM POPOV

(*taking his hand*) You've large hands. Shepherd's hands, perhaps. They might have held a flute.

POSTMASTER

Why however did you — !

MADAM POPOV

(*singing*)

> Today I'll play my flute for you.
> I've never had a kiss and so
> I'll play it low.

POSTMASTER

Remarkable! Yes I once . . a song I used to . . herding the animals. Most remarkable that you —

MADAM POPOV

MADAM POPOV

Thirty-three years. Come, shepherd, I take your hand. (*He complies dumbly, half-amused. She leads him to the painting just as she led Deetrum earlier.*) Do you like the woods? Notice the trees and birds . . the sunset.

POSTMASTER

A most excellent day by the stroke. Some painting.

MADAM POPOV

Shall we walk? My name is Vera.

POSTMASTER

My name is Hans. Although behind my desk I'm known —

MADAM POPOV

Ahh! Then I was right. You've come at last.

POSTMASTER

Come at . . I beg your . .

MADAM POPOV

To claim your little Vera.

POSTMASTER

(*catching on finally the second time around*) My little . . VERA!! You're . . you're . . You're Madam Vera Popov? Oh my God.

MADAM POPOV

Faithful Hans. You do remember.

POSTMASTER

Yes I . . No! . . Remember what?

MADAM POPOV

Me . . My father's going.

POSTMASTER

Oh no. No! I only remember . . that is —

MADAM POPOV

Yes?

POSTMASTER

Stories in the village. The drunken men . . complaining how they'd been brought here . . questioned. Of course we discounted their . . ghost tales . . since spirits were so obviously on their breath, ha ha ha. Madam Popov. Weeping Lords and Ladies, then you're real. (*He makes for the door. Deetrum and Roro appear, barring the exit.*)

MADAM POPOV

I wouldn't go just yet, Mister Postmaster. (*He turns back to the room. She nods. The servants exit.*) Look about you, Hans. These relics, this rotting furniture. I've chosen to be buried here these years because I once profaned the dictates of my heritage. Now, finally, I am to be free.

POSTMASTER

(*pause*) That's . . most interesting I'm sure. (*Hoping to keep her in reasonable spirits, he continues.*) But how was this . . was it brought about? If I may ask.

MADAM POPOV

Like all useless human seasons get brought about; by the most righteous sort of endeavor.

POSTMASTER

Dear me. (*Despite himself he eyes the other exits.*)

MADAM POPOV

A young girl is a delicate animal. A chance word, mound of rippling hair, even a passing song may live on, haunt, ripen . . leading the heart into . . extravagance.

POSTMASTER

Perhaps, yes.

MADAM POPOV

Yet what lures us is what is most real to us, is it not, Postmaster?

POSTMASTER

(*his head swimming*) In the manner of strange speaking, yes.

MADAM POPOV

Ah! I'm glad you agree.

POSTMASTER

(*defensive*) Yes, but then again perhaps I don't. I'm not up to being dogmatic one way or another. It's all very curious, of course, but I'm wondering . . why tell it to me? I'm just a poor public —

MADAM POPOV

HYPOCRITE! Because we've loved each other, you and I. We've lain together on the mosses.

POSTMASTER

Well but now just a minute here —

MADAM POPOV

Because I know every tender part and particle of your body.

POSTMASTER

Madam!

MADAM POPOV

I've offered up my brimming nakedness to you night upon night upon night.

POSTMASTER

Oh yes, yes indeed! Ha ha ha! Now if you'll excuse —

MADAM POPOV

You were to return and take me away . . or do penance for your default.

MADAM POPOV

POSTMASTER

(*at last deciding he'd best grab the initiative*) Whoa! Now, Madam, I confess I don't know how your humors actually lie in this matter. But I swear to you, here before God and my love of asparagus, I've never seen you before. Ever. Not once.

MADAM POPOV

We were to be married.

POSTMASTER

No doubt, ho ho, rings and all. Oh it's true, I used to pass the castle. And someone from a balcony sang back the stupid tunes I farrowed going to the fields. But that was all, I swear. I swear to the truth of it.

MADAM POPOV

(*quietly*) Truth is the cut our sorrows make to quell the pain. (*pause*) IN MY MIND, SHEPHERD; IN MY MIND!! Thirty years you've courted me in my mind, and you dare claim not to know me?!!

POSTMASTER

I've an idea. Why not let's let me toddle off now, please, and I'll say nothing of this to anyone.

MADAM POPOV

Have you come to take me away?

POSTMASTER

But, Madam — !

MADAM POPOV

(*most terrible of all*) THEN DO YOUR PENANCE!!!! (*Pause. When she resumes, it is quietly. No pretense or playacting, or very little.*) Sir, you're pale and shaking. You're all awobble. I'm sorry for that, truly. (*She smiles. He smiles. She chuckles. He chuckles.*) That's better, don't be frightened. Why not lie down a moment before you go? Catch your breath. It's been strange for you, I know. Just a little longer. Come, shepherd, take my hand. We're nearly through. (*Confused, but pleased at any intimation of leaving, the Postmaster complies. She leads him to the table, where he lies down.*)

POSTMASTER

Thank you. Oh yes. There . . that's better. I guessed it was a joke all along. Though you frightened me there for a moment. But I detected . . underneath.. . Oh I'm tired. All a bit queer to the humdrum, you might say.

MADAM POPOV

I'm sure it is. (*Deftly she fastens his arms to the table bucklers.*)

POSTMASTER

More playing, eh? Ha ha ha. But then you needn't have fastened . . I've not fallen from bed since my last — (*He stops, having spotted the knife above him.*) Oh my . . my . . oh my God!

MADAM POPOV

You'll be free of your petty humdrum soon enough, coward.

POSTMASTER

But I've a family! My desk and stamps. My habits.

MADAM POPOV

How I loved you once, unworthy as you were.

POSTMASTER

Who'll keep the payments and carry on?

MADAM POPOV

The weak fall first when we remake the world. The indifferent law of change.

POSTMASTER

But the world is good, Madam, where's your viewing? Why buck and bellow up a changing storm the while, when life is good!

MADAM POPOV

Life . . is stained rotten to its seeping stinking core! (*She sits on the throne, resting her head back.*)

POSTMASTER

Still this morning there were new birds on the leeward hedge, whistling at sunrise. What do you make of that . . ? We were to picnic at the dam . . capons and carrots . . Found a rare stamp for my box . . Spanish nightpost . . The flowers have burst their bloom . . the insects breeding . . Oh it was such — (*Madam Popov noticeably pushes back with her head and the knife falls.*) an excellent beginning. (*He of course dies.*)

MADAM POPOV

(*comes to him*) Forgive me, sir. But love is ever petulant. It needs must have its way at last. (*She kisses him — rather perfunctorily under the circumstances. Sits on the throne. Breathes deeply. Rings a small desk bell. No answer. A cow bell. Ditto. A dinner bell. The three servants arrive in a dead heat. Roro is first to spot the corpse. He motions, they cluster to one side.*)

RORO

Galloping entrails, she's really done it this year!

DEETRUM

He's dead? But never before —

MADAM POPOV

SPUD

Never ever. Never dead before.

MADAM POPOV

Take him to the vaults. (*Without further word they unleash the Postmaster. Spud resets the knife. Deetrum and Roro carry the Postmaster off. Spud starts after them.*) Spud . . Stay with me. (*He does, quaking with fear.*) Poor little peasant. We belong together, don't we. Two misty-eyed pups keeping company at the last. (*She examines a few objects in the room. A casual but realistic interest*) You loved the things of life once, didn't you, Spud? When you were small and . . brisk?

SPUD

Uh, why yes, Madam. Yes I did.

MADAM POPOV

(*knowing the end she is after*) The rainclaps, the clover, the moon-dogs.

SPUD

(*warming up to it*) The rooks and traprocks. The witchwoods and sneezeweeds growing.

MADAM POPOV

Perhaps a wheelhouse by the run?

SPUD

(*taking the bait, eagerly*) Yes. And the man at the millpond cried for not having crumbs enough —

MADAM POPOV

And are you happy now? (*no answer*) Of course not. Because you've been obliged to lie. (*She kisses his·cheek.*) I am tired. Help me down. (*She gives him her white shawl. He helps her up on the table.*) Death comes a-scowling everywhere in the winds now, howling after pretense. There's no dodging it. (*Spud stands bewildered.*) Sit down. (*She points to the throne. He hesitates.*) Go on. It's no matter anymore who sits where. (*He sits. Whimpers. Pause.*) I wonder if they'll ever know how much I too longed to give it up? I too. The stupid goddamned foolery. (*pause*) But lies spring quick like pokeweed in our paths; and the silences we keep are staggering. (*Spud cries openly. Madam points overhead.*) Look up there, now, Spud, you little blubbering fellow. Do you see the sky? No, not in the painting. Up, higher up. You'll have to stretch your neck back to see it.

SPUD

(*looking earnestly high overhead*) Almost . . yes . . that is, I think . . I think . .

47

MADAM POPOV

(*angrily*) Not think! Pretend! (*as before*) The sun is at zenith. There's a cloud . . like a thumping great whitefish, feeding on the fingering eelgrasses of the universe.

SPUD

Oh yes! Yes, I do see it. I do.

MADAM POPOV

(*to herself*) Good. We'll get to the flesh all right. (*continuing*) And higher up, in the clearing . . there where the winds are bolted and broken and shaken free . . comes a dumb whispering upon our ears: "Pretend you care for one another, you foundering fools."

SPUD

I hear, Madam! I hear it!

MADAM POPOV

And further on — you must press back your neck to see it — a rainbow ribbing the far horizon. Lean back . . away back. An arch bracing up the old rank boneyards of Heaven.

SPUD

(*finally leaning on the neckpiece*) Oh my yes . . gold and blue . . and the true hueing yellows! Ah such excellent . . such an excellent . . (*The knife falls.*)

MADAM POPOV

. . ending, my little shepherd. Thank God. Flesh has overcome metaphor at last. (*And she too dies, of course. Spud is stupified. He makes a lunge and happens to hang upon the dinner-bell rope, banging it terribly. Roro and Deetrum enter. Unable to speak, Spud points at Madam. Roro examines the situation, then fixes himself upon Spud, hugging him.*)

RORO

You dear sweet dimple, you've done it! You've managed it.

DEETRUM

She's dead?

RORO

Like a fish. We're free!

DEETRUM

Dead!

RORO

He's killed her. He has actually — in truth, fact, and verities — coldcocked the old girl!

48

SPUD

(*looking up*) But it was only . . I was just . . boneyards . .

RORO

Who'd have thought the least among us — (*patting Spud*) Spud, you have first dibs on the throne. Bring out the wine. No more sham. Death to pretense. (*Roro leaps and dances. Deetrum follows in his fashion. They bang and make noise, break things, give gratuitous raspberries, lie on the floor, etc.*)

DEETRUM

We'll be our own bosses. Determine our own . . what was it?

RORO

Contours and compasses! No more playacting, what a relief. (*Roro strews the contents of the trunk about the room. Spud notices the shawl which he still has in his hands. He comes to Madam, covers her with it.*)

DEETRUM

We'll sleep until noon.

RORO

Get good and drunk!

DEETRUM

Talk of old times.

RORO

Whatever we like. The cult of actual freedoms has begun! (*They hop, bounce, stomp. Spud holds up his hand like a schoolboy until the others finally see and give attention.*)

SPUD

And may I go outside the castle sometimes? (*pause*) I mean into the really world? (*pause*) I mean into the truly, truly really world?

RORO

Of course not!

DEETRUM

No need to!

RORO

(*indicating the castle*) Because now it's all ours. (*runs to the painting*) First, we tear down this damned ridiculous painting. (*They rip lustily at the huge canvas until it comes off the wall. Behind it is an obvious identical painting, minus the sun. They stand back, eyeing and admiring.*) AAAAAAAAAAAAAAAAAHHH!! Fresh air! Sea breeze off the sound. Get your corn, Spud. Let's move it. (*Spud gets the corn. Same pan ritual as at the opening of the play.*) Nothing like the elements themselves, huh, Deetrum?

49

DEETRUM

I'd forgotten what it's like. The forests and beasties! Bat calls in the gloam.

RORO

We were nearly lost. But now *we'll* decide who oils the curtains, feeds the birds, limes the vaults.

DEETRUM

Who clangs the call bells on the hour, and what we wear.

RORO

And we can paint the sun wherever we like. WHEREVER WE LIKE! (*Roro and Spud dance about with each other, drinking wine, shouting, as Deetrum joyously paints a glowing sun at midday.*)

ALL

We're free, we're free, we're free . .

CURTAIN

Madam Popov by Gladden Schrock was presented August 20, 28, and September 11, 25, 1970, at the Other Place Theatre, the experimental stage of The Guthrie Theater, Minneapolis. It was directed by Dan Bly.

Cast of Characters

MADAM POPOV	Allison Giglio
RORO	Gerry Black
SPUD	William Levis
DEETRUM	Stephen Keep
POSTMASTER	Dan Bly

THE COMPANY THEATRE ENSEMBLE
WITH SCRIPT BY DON KEITH OPPER

Children of the Kingdom

And I say unto you, That many shall come
from the east and west, and shall sit down with
Abraham, and Isaac, and Jacob, in the kingdom
of heaven.

But the children of the kingdom shall be cast
out into outer darkness: there shall be weeping
and gnashing of teeth.

Matthew 8:11–12

Cast of Characters

JASON, cameraman on the film being made of the group's tour

BILL, sound man on the film

FLASH, production manager. He is responsible for setting up equipment, light show, etc.

TOMMIE, assistant helping to set up the equipment for Frank Owens at the beginning. He is young and full of artistic naiveté. He can sing — perhaps better than Peter.

JACK, lead guitar. A frenetic, nervous, electric man-boy who has all the attributes of the instruments he plays. He talks of nothing but the guitar and rock music — these are his whole life. We cannot see him as anything but a rock musician — and neither can he.

GRANNY, rhythm guitar. A stable, long-time musician whose approach to the whole scene is a reflection of his musical function in the group. He is probably older than the others and to him rock music is just another job. He cannot understand the temper tantrums and seeming childishness around him, or his own manifestations of these.

FRANK OWENS, house manager-owner. A man concerned with time and numbers of seats. He is more likely to be into jazz than rock music. He doesn't understand why there need to be so many people involved with the group.

GALADRIEL, dancer. A harmless acid freak — totally spaced and incapable of coping with reality. She is safe in this rock world.

GREENE, bass guitar. He is into transcendental meditation and the low notes of the instrument he plays. He does what he has to and is largely unconcerned with the heaviness around him except as a phenomenon to be dealt with through meditation and thought.

PAMELA, musical leader of the groupies. She is a little older than the rest of the girls, a little more respected by the band, a little less impressed with the whole thing.

FORK, dancer. Utensil — really into the whole scene but prudish — an artiste.

52

DAVID, piano/organ. He is into classical music and is somewhat confused by the frills that accompany Peter's act. If the band were to fold he would probably concentrate on classical composition in which he indulges now only as a hobby.

MADELINE, the newest groupie. Quite carried away by the romance of it all. She has a teeny-bopper mouth, talks all the time, is a lousy lay but thinks she's great.

FREDDIE, secretary to Alan Weeks. An efficiency expert who does exactly what she is told and is helpless unless someone directs her. She is always busy taking care of business and details.

JOANNE, Peter's old lady. She has been through it all with him — perhaps even went to high school with him and helped him even then with the writing of his songs. She knows he will always fuck around with other girls, and she will stand by him through his escapades but not without a certain resistance. She is closer to him than anyone else with the possible exception of Michael with whom she is good friends.

ALICIA, Granny's wife. She almost never stays for the concerts but catches a movie instead. She is unconcerned with the hubbub and would much rather be at home with her children, although she is congenial in every way. She and Joanne are good friends.

HONEY, drummer. An unapproachable — perhaps even hostile — character who met Peter in jail. His relationship with Peter is one of mutual respect and admiration which transcends the realm of the rock-music scene. He seems to have an antipathy for Joanne and Michael.

BONNIE, the public relations lady (alias Superwoman). She is genuinely in love with the rock scene and has found a place for herself in this regime. She is always in evidence at the concerts and seems completely out of place in this environment of freaks, though she, too, is a kind of freak. In matters of business she is totally competent and handles herself with professional aplomb. A motherly concern for the individuals of the group may be apparent.

MICHAEL, an old friend of Peter's. He is the head man who takes care of the dope and the religious needs of the group. He should be totally capable of handling any situation

— either with words of advice or vials of cocaine. He is on friendly terms with all members of the group except Honey.

MARK MATTHEWS, television reporter

HARRY RANDALL, newspaper reporter

ALAN WEEKS, business manager of the group. He controls the money and the contracts. On the surface he seems to be looking out for the good of the group — and Peter in particular — but at base is only interested in money. Human beings are instruments to him and must be handled accordingly in order for them to be productive.

ANNIE, Peter's newest flame. She is the portrait of newness, especially to Peter. She is the leader of the groupies because of her current favor with Peter, and because of this also her relationship with Joanne is understandably strained. Annie constantly milks the prestigious position she holds.

PETER, lead singer. He is a man with an empire — a man with a notoriety that is almost religious in nature. People obey him with a smile. He is quiet and withdrawn into his work. He is isolated and must wage the classic losing battle against fate from this position.

(NOTE: This play is a tragedy. It is concerned with the death of heroes. Our hero's death is the inevitable result of forces leading him toward his fate — his band, his friends, his business associates, and especially his audience. All individuals in the hero's milieu are involved with him parasitically, and it is clear that he is being destroyed by the image over whose structuring he has had no control and by which he now finds himself defined. Multiple-focus scenes and unexpected locale transitions should combine to both define and implicate the audience as an integral part of the action.)

CHILDREN OF THE KINGDOM

ACT ONE

As the audience enters Flash, Tommie, and Jack are onstage or throughout the house. Jack and Tommie are balancing equipment while Flash is fooling with the lights. There should be many light changes as the audience enters; some houselights are on, some off. Entrances in this scene are made from every available door.

JACK
(*singing*) Hey, baby, I'm callin' from the jail . .

TOMMIE
What is that?

JACK
A song.

TOMMIE
Song. (*putters around*)

JACK
New one . . I think we'll do it while we're here.

FLASH
(*to Jack*) Move around a bit. (*under some kind of lighting*) The other way. Good, move around a bit more. Okay. (*lighting and technical dialogue to be inserted by the players until Granny enters*)

GRANNY
(*enters eating a sandwich and perhaps singing the national anthem*) How'd we get booked in here?

JACK
Whataya talking about.

Lyrics by Don Keith Opper, Jack Rowe, Bob Walter, and Wiley Rinaldi.

GRANNY
Shitty little seats . .

FLASH
(*from the booth*) You should see the shitty wiring.

JACK
Give me an ''E.''

GRANNY
(*like a cheer*) ''E.''

JACK
Come on. I want to get this done.

GRANNY
(*gives him an ''E''*) Is that right?

JACK
I don't know.

GRANNY
Where's David?

JACK
I don't know that either.

GRANNY
What are you coming down off of this time?

JACK
I'm not coming down off anything.

GRANNY
The evil cocaine . .

JACK
(*finally admits it*) I confess . . (*Owens enters.*)

OWENS
We gonna be on time?

GRANNY
Our people'll be ready.

OWENS
Fine. Is Mr. Weeks here yet?

GRANNY
I don't think so.

JACK
He's having a late lunch.

OWENS
What . .

GRANNY
Don't worry. He'll be here. He likes to check everything beforehand.

CHILDREN OF THE KINGDOM

JACK

Everything beforehand. (*Galadriel comes tripping in with a small book of poetry. Greene follows her in, letting her do whatever she wants but watching that she doesn't hurt herself. Owens is looking with suspicion.*)

GREENE

(*to Owens*) It's okay. She's with us.

OWENS

For your own good . . don't dope in here.

JACK

Of course not.

GREENE

Oh, she's not doped.

GRANNY

Of course not.

JACK

She's a dope.

OWENS

Of course not. Just remember what I said. The police don't care who you are.

GALADRIEL

(*to Owens*) How do you do?

OWENS

Hello. What do you do with the group?

GALADRIEL

Uh . .

GREENE

She's a dancer . . a very fine dancer. Right?

JACK

The finest.

OWENS

(*doesn't believe a word of it*) Okay. I can tell. (*goes off talking about something completely different*) Tell Weeks I'll be in the office and keep her out of the light booth.

JACK

Okay.

GREENE

(*to Owens*) Greene. (*to Jack*) How are we on time?

JACK

We're okay.

GALADRIEL

What about time?

COMPANY THEATRE ENSEMBLE AND DON KEITH OPPER

JACK

It's flying out the window.

GREENE

Jack . .

JACK

Okay. It's not flying out the window.

GALADRIEL

Where does it go?

JACK

It . . I don't know. Greene, get her away from me.

GALADRIEL

Where's Peter?

GRANNY

He'll be here. (*Pamela and Fork enter together and meet Galadriel with some concern.*)

PAMELA

Where have you been?

GALADRIEL

I went for a walk.

JACK

(*to Granny*) Give me a "D."

GRANNY

(*does so*) Is that right?

GREENE

What time is it?

GRANNY

An hour earlier than real time.

GREEN

What?

GRANNY

Seven.

GREENE

Oh, we have time. (*David enters with some charts and a jug of water.*)

JACK

Good. Sit down and give me a "D."

DAVID

What? (*plays something*)

JACK

No. No. Just one "D." (*David does so. They tune for a while.*)

PAMELA

You can't just go wandering off like that. I knew something would happen.

CHILDREN OF THE KINGDOM

GALADRIEL

Oh, he was very nice to me.

FORK

Why shouldn't he be?

JACK

She's happy. What's the big deal?

PAMELA

Somebody took advantage of her.

JACK

But she's happy.

FORK

But not really.

JACK

Of course not really. How could anyone be happy really?

GALADRIEL

That's exactly right.

JACK

I know it is. I've been saying . . oh shit. Who am I talking to? (*Madeline and Freddie enter.*)

GALADRIEL

I've been trying to tell you that . . Hello, hello. Look at this book Peter bought me.

PAMELA

A book? Let me see. It's very nice. (*They all treat Galadriel grandly.*)

MADELINE

(*to Freddie*) I have no idea what he's doing now. He told me that he couldn't stay where he was and didn't know how to leave.

FORK

Who are you talking about?

MADELINE

You don't know him.

FREDDIE

So what happened to him?

MADELINE

I left him before he decided. I don't know what he did after that.

FREDDIE

He was a great guitarist.

GRANNY

Terry Tainly.

MADELINE

How do you know him?

FORK

I do too know him.

GRANNY

I just know him.

MADELINE

What's he doing now?

GRANNY

What's the difference? (*goes back to tuning*)

PAMELA

He bought a farm.

MADELINE

A farm?

PAMELA

That's what I heard.

MADELINE

A lot of good guitar going to waste.

FREDDIE

You can't be sure. (*Joanne and Alicia enter.*)

GRANNY

(*to Alicia*) Mother of pearl. (*to Joanne*) Howya doin'?

JOANNE

Okay.

GRANNY

Where is Peter?

JOANNE

Sulking.

GRANNY

What's the matter now?

JOANNE

Nobody knows.

ALICIA

He's up and down — up and down. You know . .

GRANNY

Did you talk to him?

ALICIA

A little bit. We gotta get him to lay off the coke for a while.

GRANNY

Could be. I'll have to talk to Michael about that. (*Jack and David begin to rehearse very loud. Owens enters.*)

OWENS

(*to Greene*) Who are all these people?

CHILDREN OF THE KINGDOM

GREENE
Part of the group.

OWENS
All these people?

GREENE
Sure. (*taking him to Galadriel*) You've met Galadriel . .

OWENS
Yes.

GREENE
And this is Fork . . who was just going out for lunch. She sings backup for us . . a valuable girl, Fork. And this is Pamela. Pamela, this is Mr. Owens. Yes, and this is Madeline, and this is Alicia, Granny's wife . . this is Mr. Owens . . and Granny, and next to him here is Joanne . . and this is Honey Carswell, going right by . . He's very busy you know . . and David, over there . . and Jack . . I'd like to introduce . .

JACK
Jack Gordon. I'm with the Post Office Department.

GREENE
Lead guitar . . Frank Owens.

JACK
Are we going to do something here or not?

DAVID
Peter's not here yet.

OWENS
Is he going to be late?

DAVID
No, not a thing to worry about.

OWENS
'Cause I've got a full house, you know.

GREENE
Don't worry about a thing. (*Freddie and Owens exit.*)

JOANNE
I don't know. I'm tired of it. Flying from one town to another . . Peter treating me like . .

ALICIA
I'm tired too.

GRANNY
We're all tired. I mean Peter too. He's tired.

ALICIA
Living out of a suitcase. I could be home . .

JOANNE

You've got a place to go. This (*indicates the theatre*) is all I have. Take a look. Shit.

GRANNY

Come on. Knock it off.

ALICIA

When this madness stops . .

GRANNY

It's fatigue. Believe me, that's all. Nothing to worry about.

DAVID

Are we going to rehearse or not?

JACK

YEAH. (*Honey enters.*)

GRANNY

(*to Honey*) Hey, fucker . .

HONEY

(*to Granny*) Hello, asshole. (*sits down and begins to rap out something on the drums, interrupting everyone*)

GRANNY

Sounds like sponges.

HONEY

What do you know about it?

GRANNY

I know they don't sound right. I'll be back.

JACK

Get me a beer.

PAMELA

(*to Madeline*) No, it's not that. I've known other people like him before. He just seems a bit different.

MADELINE

They're all the same . . all the same. (*Bonnie enters.*) All the same. Bonnie . . Bonnie, can we try new dresses tonight? I picked one up . .

BONNIE

Wait a minute. Has everyone got here? Where's Annie?

MADELINE

Where do you think?

BONNIE

I don't know. That's why I asked.

MADELINE

She's with Peter.

CHILDREN OF THE KINGDOM

BONNIE

When did that start?

MADELINE

Couple days ago.

JOANNE

(*to Madeline*) Say . . that's just charming. Just charming. (*Alicia and Joanne exit.*)

JACK

(*to Bonnie*) Hey, Superwoman . . hey, hey, Superwoman . .

BONNIE

Hello, hello. Where's Granny and . .

GREENE

Granny went to get Jack a beer.

BONNIE

And Peter?

GREENE

He's late.

MADELINE

Anyway, can we get an advance on salary for these new . .

BONNIE

I'll have to talk to Alan.

MADELINE

Shit, I'll talk to Peter.

HONEY

What in the world is this . . place?

DAVID

(*walking through the house*) A nice enough place. A lot quieter out here.

BONNIE

Honey, have you seen Peter?

HONEY

Well, to tell the truth, no.

FREDDIE

Do you have any idea where he might be?

HONEY

No.

JACK

Somebody got a cigarette?

MADELINE

I do. (*pause . . waiting*)

JACK

Are we gonna do something here or not? (*Michael enters.*) Michael, Michael. Come right over here, you dear boy.

BONNIE

Michael, where is he? You've talked to him? (*Michael nods and goes to Jack.*)

FREDDIE

Everybody — everybody. Here are little name tags that say that you're with us . . so they won't throw us out. If you get any hassle whatever, talk to me or Bonnie. Here you are. Here's yours . .

DAVID

Next thing we'll have to wear uniforms.

JACK

Oh, my own little name tag. Isn't that cute.

HONEY

What is that?

FREDDIE

Name tag.

HONEY

I know my name. (*Madeline and Pamela exit. Galadriel wanders in unattended with some weed.*)

GALADRIEL

Here. (*She is giving it out.*) Here . . for you . . for you . .

DAVID

Help!

FREDDIE

What is she doing?

MICHAEL

It's grass.

JACK

Gimme some of that.

HONEY

Get it away from that chick. We'll all end up in jail.

JACK

Take it away from her and give it to me.

BONNIE

Throw it away.

JACK

THROW IT AWAY???

HONEY

There's no need to throw it away.

CHILDREN OF THE KINGDOM

MICHAEL

Galadriel, give me what you have. Come on, I'll hold it for you . . that's it . .

GALADRIEL

Isn't it nice the way it's rolled?

MICHAEL

Who gave it to you?

GALADRIEL

I don't know.

JACK

What's the difference?

GREENE

Galadriel, you can't hand dope out like that.

GALADRIEL

Why?

HONEY

Because you'll get us all busted, you dumb cunt.

GREENE

You'll get arrested.

GALADRIEL

Why?

JACK

What are you talking to her for? Just give me some of it.

MICHAEL

I've got it. I've got the coke, too. Do you want some of it now?

JACK

Now? I don't know. I guess we could go in the bathroom.

MICHAEL

Okay.

GALADRIEL

Where are you going?

JACK

I've got to help Michael go to the bathroom. (*They go into the bathroom. Greene takes Galadriel out. Weeks enters.*)

BONNIE

(*to Weeks*) I'm glad you're here. Peter's not here.

WEEKS

I just talked to him.

BONNIE

Everything is . . ?

WEEKS

Fine. Everything's fine.

DAVID

Is he here?

WEEKS

He's in the dressing room.

DAVID

We're ready to rehearse. (*Jack wanders out of the bathroom stoned out. Greene comes in at the same time.*)

JACK

That sure beats Dristan.

WEEKS

What's the matter with him?

BONNIE

Well . .

MICHAEL

He's responding well to treatment.

DAVID

(*to Jack*) You're all right?

JACK

Of course I'm all right.

GREENE

(*disgusted*) Oh, man . .

JACK

(*to Greene*) Hey, man, really, it's okay.

GREENE

It's not okay.

MICHAEL

It's okay.

GREENE

We got a show to do.

JACK

I'm all right.

GREENE

It's not all right. (*Madeline, Pamela, and Fork enter.*)

JACK

(*to Weeks*) What's up, Money?

WEEKS

You together?

JACK

Me? Sure. Glued together.

MADELINE

Glued together again.

PAMELA

(*to Fork*) I can't figure him out.

FORK

Figure him out? I love him.

PAMELA

You love him?

FORK

Look at that guitar.

BONNIE

We're ready to go here, Alan.

WEEKS

Fine. Where's Owens?

BONNIE

I don't know.

PAMELA

So what? Anybody can play the guitar.

FORK

Not like him.

PAMELA

So what? (*Owens enters.*)

OWENS

Mr. Weeks. Mr. Weeks . . (*Galadriel enters.*)

GALADRIEL

STOP! STOP!

HONEY

Shut up.

GALADRIEL

I'm going to give the prayer.

HONEY

Fuck the prayer.

MICHAEL

Let her do it.

GREENE

Okay. Come on, Galadriel's giving a prayer.

JACK

This is crazy.

GALADRIEL

All right, let's have a little respect.

PAMELA

Galadriel . .

FORK

Let her do it.

WEEKS

What is this?

GREENE

The prayer.

WEEKS

I've got business to . .

GREENE

Can it wait for one moment? Go ahead.

GALADRIEL

Oh most holy Polyhymnia
We who prepare to honor thee
And all thy billowed riches
Ask only for thy blessing
On this house and all who enter our . .

WEEKS

Good. Now . . Mr. Owens . .

GALADRIEL

I haven't finished.

WEEKS

I don't have the time . .

GALADRIEL

I'm not finished.

WEEKS

Look, we've got things . . (*Galadriel begins to cry.*)

GALADRIEL

You've interrupted the prayer. You've interrupted the priestess. This can only mean . . it's your fault. If disaster falls on our humble heads it's all your fault.

GREENE

It's okay, Galadriel. Hey, it's okay.

GALADRIEL

No, it isn't. You should know that. And it's his fault.

WEEKS

This is ridiculous.

MADELINE

It was wonderful, Galadriel.

CHILDREN OF THE KINGDOM

GALADRIEL

No . . (*Galadriel, Greene, Fork, and Madeline exit.*)

OWENS

She's a dancer?

WEEKS

Well, you know what . .

OWENS

Sure, sure. Anyway, we have a full house for you for the entire run.

WEEKS

Really? Very good. (*The following speeches, until the voice comes from the back, overlap.*)

BONNIE

Mr. Owens isn't used to running houses this large.

WEEKS

Then it's a pleasant surprise I'm sure . .

JACK

Let's get going on this thing.

OWENS

Rowdy kids.

WEEKS

Perhaps you should hire some police.

OWENS

No, I wouldn't want to do that.

DAVID

Are we going to rehearse or not?

HONEY

Yeah, come on.

OWENS

(*as they walk toward the back*) We can talk in the office.

WEEKS

That'll be fine. (*Someone hollers from the back.*)

VOICE

Telephone call for Alan Weeks. Is he here?

WEEKS

What is it?

VOICE

Long distance . .

WEEKS

Okay. (*Weeks goes to pick up the call. Granny enters from the direction of the call.*)

GRANNY

Hey, this is it.

DAVID

Toronto?

JACK

Where's my beer?

GRANNY

Shut up. (*They are trying to listen to the conversation on the telephone.*)

JACK

I asked you to get me a beer.

GRANNY

SHHHHH. (*Weeks is overheard.*)

WEEKS

Yeah, Barney, how are you? . . Yeah, I know. Oh, yeah. GOOD . . Where? . . That's a pretty big place . . No, I'm not worried about it . . It's just that . . well, you know. It's our biggest yet. Sure . . the band can handle it. Sure they're that good . . don't you listen to the radio? Yeah, I know . . No, you know, this boy of mine . . will knock that town over. Well, I'm glad . . yeah . . a step along the road toward success, right? (*laughs*) Sure. Okay, we'll make the final arrangements next week. I'm flying up Thursday . . Okay . . Yes, I love talking to you but the phone call is costing you money . . Barney? (*During the phone call Peter enters with Annie.*)

PETER

What is that?

GRANNY

Yeah.

DAVID

Glad to see you, Peter.

PETER

Sorry I'm late. (*Madeline, Galadriel, Pamela, and Fork enter.*)

MADELINE

Annie, you dear girl, you.

ANNIE

What?

DAVID

Are we going to rehearse or not?

GRANNY

(*to Peter*) Are we?

PETER

I don't think so.

CHILDREN OF THE KINGDOM

BONNIE

WHAT? We've got to.

PETER

Maybe a bit.

BONNIE

I've got the press coming.

JACK

Now where's Greene?

HONEY

If you guys ever get it together send me a telegram.

PAMELA

The girls need rehearsal.

PETER

Take them into a dressing room.

ANNIE

He doesn't talk much. I don't really know . .

PAMELA

Come on . .

ANNIE

Really, I don't know yet.

DAVID

Locked away in a little room full of these chicks?

GRANNY

Have you seen the dressing rooms? (*Michael saunters up to Peter.*)

MICHAEL

Aren't you Penis Corman? Listen, a chick out front offered me twenty-five dollars for three pubic hairs.

PETER

Twenty-five dollars apiece, or for all three? (*Galadriel enters tossing flower petals.*)

GALADRIEL

Hosannah . . hosannah . . hosannah.

PETER

(*to Galadriel*) How are you, Sister?

GALADRIEL

What troubles you, Peter? (*Weeks enters.*)

WEEKS

Peter . .

PETER

Well, speak of the devil . .

GALADRIEL

(*to Weeks*) There's a small problem with the plumbing in the hallway.

WEEKS

Then why don't you go say a prayer? (*Galadriel is withdrawn by Greene.*) I closed the deal for Toronto.

PETER

Toronto?

GRANNY

I told you . .

PETER

I hate Toronto.

WEEKS

How do you like twelve thousand dollars?

PETER

Not as much as I hate Toronto.

GRANNY

Just go and sign whatever you have to sign. We're going.

WEEKS

It's the Commonwealth Auditorium.

PETER

Really.

WEEKS

Really. (*exits*)

JACK

Peter, can I talk to you for a second? (*holds up a guitar*) I have this on what they call approval . . now, I approve. What I need is . .

PETER

. . the final approval.

JACK

Right. (*Jack and Peter exit. The news media men enter. Freddie and Bonnie intercept them.*)

BONNIE

Gentlemen . .

NEWS I

When does the rehearsal . .

NEWS II

There was supposed to be a rehearsal . .

BONNIE

Gentlemen . .

FREDDIE

I told them that it was . .

CHILDREN OF THE KINGDOM

BONNIE

It was just beautiful. Sorry you didn't get here on time.

NEWS I

But she said that it was called off . .

BONNIE

Nonsense. You must have misunderstood. We waited as long as we could . .

NEWS II

We were told to be here at seven.

BONNIE

That's when it ended.

NEWS I

I was supposed to have an interview with Peter Corman . . (*News II spots Granny and begins to question him.*)

GRANNY

I have no idea, man.

NEWS II

You must have some idea.

GRANNY

No, none. I just work here. Say, who are you?

NEWS II

I'm the Madman Mark Matthews from KCTW.

GRANNY

Well, how do you do? My name's Granville Turner. I play the bagpipes with this band.

FREDDIE

Uh, about your interview with Mr. Corman . .

NEWS II

Oh, Mr. Corman . .

BONNIE

Gentlemen . .

NEWS I

Look, we were promised interviews. There's a story here.

FREDDIE

You'll get your interviews.

BONNIE

But as you can see, it will be impossible for you both to interview everyone in the group.

NEWS I

I'd like to see Peter Corman.

BONNIE

I'm *sure* you would.

NEWS II

I'm supposed to get Corman.

BONNIE

But as you can see, he isn't here.

NEWS I

What about the drummer? I'll take the drummer.

FREDDIE

The drummer isn't exactly . .

BONNIE

. . here at the moment . .

NEWS II

Look, we were told . .

BONNIE

I know and we will arrange something. Peter, however, has requested that he does not see reporters before a show. And Honey . .

NEWS I

Honey? The new sex angle, the new chick. Who's Honey?

FREDDIE

The drummer.

NEWS I

Oh, well, I wanted him. I was told to get him.

BONNIE

If you had been here on time . .

NEWS II

We were told to be here at seven and . .

BONNIE

You were told wrong. Now you'll just have to be content with audience reaction or whatever until I can arrange something else. I can say this, however: Peter might consent to be interviewed by one reporter after the show, but not by both of you. So you'd better decide between yourselves who that one will be. Honey, on the other hand, will not tolerate reporters, and that's all there is to it. And I wouldn't suggest busting in on him either, because . .

FREDDIE

You'd better stay away from Honey for your own good.

GRANNY

Hey, I'll tell you what. You want to see Honey, right? What you do is, you get a big piece of raw meat, open his dressing room door, and toss it in . . (*Granny exits.*)

BONNIE

The others are quite amiable to reporters and will give you good stories, I'm sure.

74

CHILDREN OF THE KINGDOM

NEWS I

I'll take Corman.

NEWS II

What? Horseshit . .

NEWS I

Look, you can have all the rest . .

NEWS II

All the rest? But I came here to get Corman. (*to Bonnie*) Look, when can we get going on these things?

BONNIE

Just as soon as possible. But right now we have a show to do, remember? Freddie . . (*Bonnie and Freddie exit. This should leave only the news media men who are bantering back and forth about interviews and into tape recorders. They begin interviewing the audience. This is the first time that the audience has been recognized as being there. The questions should be concerned with how they came to be at the theatre, have they ever been to rock concerts before, which ones, etc., etc. After a few moments the houselights dim and the band comes onstage. As the music starts,* so does the light show. We are now at a rock concert.*)

OWENS

(*over the loudspeaker*) Ladies and Gentlemen: ACE HANNAH.

ACE HANNAH with PETER

Lady of the Billboard

I was driving down a side street
looking for a woman to fill my needs.
Like a farmer in Ohio
I need somewhere to plant my seed.
When there she was, a woman
who could just about bed me to death
selling Scotch on the corner
in a low-cut see-through dress.
I asked her where're you going
"America" 's what she said.
I bet that around the corner
woulda done just fine instead.

She hopped down off the billboard
and squeezed into my car,

---

* Inquiries concerning the music may be directed to the Company Theatre Foundation, 1024 South Robertson Boulevard, Los Angeles, California 90035.

75

twenty-two feet of woman
and enough whiskey to stock a bar.
By the time we reached the freeway
she took some liberties with my head.
She was moving real slow next to me,
like a blonde spider in her web,
and whispered "Buy this bottle, boy,
and then we'll go to bed."

I did not have the money
so we bargained for my ring.
We seemed to be all right
but then again, it wasn't everything
and I wanted her real bad,
so I offered her my Ford
which she took so breathlessly
just like it was a chore.
And when I went to collect
she smiled and said, "I'm bored."

She's my lady of the billboard,
metallic lady of the night.
My lady of the billboard
with a steel trap to hold you tight.

Queen Anne

Queen Anne sold
the mystery of day
and the reason for the night.
And though the price she asked was steep
she got it when she tried.
Within her bower of evergreen
she reclined upon her throne.
And as her court laughed behind their fans
she dazzled him.
Her beauty shone —
a golden cord
that tied him blind.

To reach his goal
he was given many tasks
that she had set for him.
He was soon reduced to rags

76

but still he waited on her whims.
He sketched her portrait
on the northern winds,
and reaped the forest made of stone,
he dug a tunnel to rainbow's end
and then returned
but all she said
was: "Where's the gold
you promised me?"

And when at last
sufficient proof
had been given of his love
she called him smiling to her side
saying, "You have done enough."
So in their passion
he spent his strength
and listened to her moan.
But as they lay there he realized
he'd signed his soul
for something that
he'd always known
the answer to.

I love you, Anne.

(As "Queen Anne" ends the lights black out and we hear the following over the loudspeakers.)

PETER

Flash, let's hear the end of that back.

FLASH

Okay. Let me rewind.

PETER

I'm gonna come up to the booth. *(The lights come up and we are in a recording studio. Peter and David exit to go to the control booth. All sound onstage that is to be heard is spoken into the microphones. Otherwise the lines are mimed. The sound from the booth is also over microphones. The effect is to put the audience into the control booth looking through the glass into the recording studio. The ending lines of "Queen Anne" are heard. Jason, Bill, and Bonnie enter the studio.)*

BONNIE

(over the microphone) I've got the review. *(The music stops.)*

77

PETER

(from the booth) What? *(The dialogue until Tommie enters must be spoken near a microphone or directly into one.)*

BONNIE

I've got the review of last night's show.

PETER

Does it say anything?

BONNIE

Sure. Do you want me to read it?

PETER

Yeah.

BONNIE

(begins reading) "Last night, this reporter was treated to one of the most exciting nights of rock that he has experienced. Ace Hannah, a band composed of five lively musicians, a host of colorful and alluring girls, a traveling light show, and lead singer Peter Corman, left the full house at Frank Owens' Light House Auditorium screaming for more. Most notable was Corman, who is gruff and sometimes vulgar, perhaps a bit too self-involved. But his steady strength rectifies his excesses . ."

PETER

That's enough.

BONNIE

There's just a bit more. Let's see ". . his excesses . . We can expect more excitement from a group with such strength and ability. Do yourself a favor and go see them."

PETER

Who wrote that?

BONNIE

E. B. W.

GRANNY

That's a bunch of shit.

PETER

I wonder if the guy was even here last night. It was a shitty show.

BONNIE

It was not.

PETER

Yes it was. The only thing the people were screaming for was their money back. It was a turk.

BONNIE

Well, I liked it.

JACK

You like them all.

BONNIE

Well, the audience liked it too.

PETER

What do they know?

GRANNY

You know they don't know what's happening with us.

BONNIE

They liked it. (*Overlaps with mimed speeches below – mimed because they are not spoken near enough to a microphone to be picked up. Tommie enters carrying a recording tape.*)

JACK

(*mimed*) Hey, you made it.

TOMMIE

(*mimed*) Yeah.

JACK

(*mimed*) Did you bring it?

TOMMIE

(*mimed*) Yeah.

JACK

(*into microphone*) Okay. Let's give it a go. Hey, Peter, I got something I want you to hear. I'll bring it up. Tommie, this is Peter.

TOMMIE

(*into microphone*) How ya doin' . .

PETER

(*from booth*) Fine. What do you do?

TOMMIE

I set up your equipment.

PETER

No, I mean on the tape.

TOMMIE

Oh, I sing.

JACK

He sings.

GRANNY

A singer, eh?

BONNIE

What else?

TOMMIE

Well, that's about all I do . . you know . .

PETER

Forget her. She's only kidding.

TOMMIE

Yeah, okay.

PETER

Where'd you meet Jack?

TOMMIE

Well, I was setting up your equipment . . I work for Owens, see . . and we got high . .

PETER

You got high with Frank Owens?

TOMMIE

No, no — I got high with Jack. And then . .

PETER

How long you been at it?

TOMMIE

Oh, I've been getting high for . .

PETER

No, no. Singing.

TOMMIE

Oh. About three years. I started with a group called 100% Beef.

PETER

Out of Chicago?

TOMMIE

Yeah.

GRANNY

I heard of them. They — uh — disbanded, didn't they?

TOMMIE

Well, not exactly. You see, the lead guitarist died of an overdose . . and after that . . well, you know, we got hassled all the time by the cops . . and that just about finished it.

PETER

Well, we can sympathize with that. Listen, we're gonna run your tape now. (The tape goes on — "Greasy Spoon" — and everyone stops to listen. The song and the singer are good. By the end of the song they should have a silent rapport with Tommie that recognizes a talent going in the same direction. The tape ends. During the song Jack, Peter, and David reenter the studio.)

CHILDREN OF THE KINGDOM

TAPE: TOMMIE and JACK

Greasy Spoon

My place is open now for business,
I call it the Greasy Spoon.
Every day the doors are open
twelve midnight 'til noon.
Don't bother knocking
'cause you know there ain't no door.
Come in and seat yourself
somewhere on the floor
and wait for me
and I'll be with you.

There's something here for you to play with,
there's something here to eat.
Forget about the salt and pepper,
just you give it heat.
The pipes are leaking
and the wind comes through the door.
Don't think of leaving
'cause you'll soon be wanting more
of coming down on me.

chorus:
Come on girl and get it.
There's something here for you.
You'll never forget it.
I'll teach you how to do it now.

PETER
(*calls to the booth; all lines may be said aloud now*) Flash?

FLASH
That enough?

PETER
Yeah, cut it off.

FLASH
That came out pretty good for a rough tape.

PETER
Yeah, it did.

BONNIE
I liked it.

81

JACK

Maybe we could use him.

GRANNY

Hey, Jack, lay back a little . .

TOMMIE

I still need work, I know.

PETER

You need work, man? How about a little backup?

TOMMIE

For you guys? (*Peter nods.*) Well, yeah . .

GRANNY

(*to Peter*) You better talk to Alan about this.

PETER

Alan works for us.

GRANNY

That's why he works for us — to hassle out the salary shit.

TOMMIE

Oh, you can forget the pay . .

PETER

You'll get paid. (*to Granny*) I'll pay him myself.

GRANNY

Okay. It's your pocket.

PETER

(*to Tommie*) How about going over a couple of things right now?

TOMMIE

Oh, I'd like to, but I'm still working for Owens. I'll have to tell him. You want me to sing tonight?

PETER

Sure.

TOMMIE

Well, are you gonna be there a little early?

PETER

Are we?

DAVID

Sure, why not — a couple of hours . .

TOMMIE

Good. Real good.

PETER

And we can talk later, maybe. (*introduces Tommie to the band*)

TOMMIE

(*to Jack*) Thanks, man. (*Tommie exits with Bonnie.*)

CHILDREN OF THE KINGDOM

GRANNY

How the fuck is he gonna sing backup?

JACK

He'll pick it up.

PETER

If he can't sing backup tonight, maybe he'll do a song.

GRANNY

What song?

PETER

I dunno. The one on the tape sounded pretty good.

HONEY

What?

GRANNY

That's unnecessary.

PETER

It's only maybe.

GRANNY

I've seen people freeze up in front of audiences. He may not be able to sing live. It's a big risk.

PETER

We should take more risks.

DAVID

Where's my water jug?

HONEY

I drank it.

DAVID

All of it?

HONEY

I thought it was gin.

GRANNY

I don't know why you have to pick up stragglers.

PETER

Stragglers?

GRANNY

You got those . . girls the same way.

PETER

I got the.band the same way.

GRANNY

But who is he?

PETER

Who are we? You heard the tape. The kid can sing. We can use him.

GRANNY

For what?

PETER

For backup. Let's get to work.

GRANNY

Yeah, but we can't go around spreading ourselves too thin.

PETER

We'll all be good together.

GREENE

That's right.

GRANNY

Look, are you planning on leaving?

PETER

No.

GRANNY

Then he's an extravagance.

DAVID

What's the matter with extravagance?

PETER

Yeah, it's an extravagance to do live performances, but we do them.

DAVID

That's right — we make a lot more money in the studio. Besides, some of those girls can't sing worth shit.

GRANNY

More stragglers.

PETER

More freaks.

GRANNY

That's all we need — more freaks.

PETER

I've been thinking it over, Granny, and that's exactly what we need — more freaks.

DAVID

What kind of freaks?

PETER

You know, like trapeze artists . . and high-wire cats.

GRANNY

If this Tommie cat can swing around on a trapeze, play the guitar, and beat off at the same time, *I'll* pay the son of a bitch.

PETER

I'm serious. Those trapeze guys are in a special place.

CHILDREN OF THE KINGDOM

GRANNY

Who said that this guy is like that? Look, it's a real risk.

PETER

Shit. It's no risk at all. What happens if the guy fucks up? Nothing. And we should be in that kind of place — all of us.

DAVID

What kind of place?

PETER

The place where if a guy fucks up it not only fucks up the act, but it kills him.

HONEY

Audiences love it when it's *that* dangerous.

PETER

Right. Hey, remember that cat who rode the bike at the pier?

HONEY

Yeah, this cat rode a bike in a round drum, you know, the kind of thing where the faster you go, the higher you go up the side of the drum. So that when you were going fast enough you were horizontal with the ground.

PETER

It was a dangerous thing.

HONEY

Yeah, real dangerous. Anyway, the people, the customers, the audience was standing above him, looking down on him going around the sides of this drum, and they'd holler: "Take off your helmet, you sissy." "Take off your goggles, you chicken." Anyway, pretty soon guys started dropping things on him, chicks would blow their compacts out on him so the powder would get in his eyes . . and cats were still yelling for him to take his helmet off. And he kept on riding through all this shit . . and he hated all those fuckers because of what they were doing to him . . he really hated them.

PETER

But . .

HONEY

But by the end he took off his helmet and took off his goggles and went riding up the sides of that drum like a maniac. And he didn't know why . . and he hated those people . . but he did it.

GRANNY

I bet he quit finally.

PETER

So what?

GRANNY

He quit before it killed him.

HONEY

That wasn't the reason he quit.

PETER

It doesn't matter why he quit.

HONEY

And it finally didn't matter what the audience wanted.

GRANNY

So what does this have to do with Tommie-boy here?

PETER

I'm talking about a place that we should shoot for — a place where we could do anything. Only the music would keep us from falling off the earth.

DAVID

I wouldn't mind being in that kind of place.

PETER

I mean, Porky Pig could walk in here and ask to play saxophone and it wouldn't faze us.

DAVID

Porky Pig?

PETER

Yeah, Porky Pig. We could send him into Weeks's Office. Can you imagine a two-dimensional pig with a bow tie and a saxophone walking into Alan's office and asking for an audition? Weeks would go out of his mind. But not us. We could sit down and talk to Porky.

HONEY

Because that pig is a celebrity.

PETER

He's got to have some interesting things to say. You gotta admit he'd have a different point of view.

GRANNY

Who gives a shit what Porky has to say?

HONEY

Maybe he's queer.

PETER

Yeah, wouldn't that be something.

GRANNY

So what?

PETER

I just want to be ready in case Porky Pig walks in here and wants to play sax.

CHILDREN OF THE KINGDOM

GRANNY

It sounds like a lot of shit to me. We got to be thinking about eating, fucking, and making good music — not Porky Pig.

PETER

You ought to give Porky a little thought, Granny. A slight case of the crazies at this point in the game wouldn't hurt.

GREENE

(*out of nowhere*) Do you think those trapeze guys think they're taking risks?

DAVID

No, but the audience does. The audience has to think that the guy's going to end up maimed or dead or at least a cripple . . and that's what makes it exciting.

GRANNY

All this talk about mutilation has made me hungry. Does anyone want to get something to eat?

DAVID

I need a drink.

GRANNY

Well, let's go.

JACK

Hey, those chicks are coming in ten minutes. (*They begin to exit with some commotion.*) Flash, we'll be back to do that track in about ten minutes. (*They exit talking about a multitude of things. During a pause Honey beats something out on the drums.*)

HONEY

Man, you've got a bunch of insurance agents for friends. They're all stuck in their jobs. They don't want to move.

PETER

(*mumbles in assent*) Stuck.

HONEY

But I've been thinking it over. Thinking about a cure. What we do is, we get them a little bust — say for pot — a couple of months in jail — that'd put their heads through some changes. And then you and me, baby, we put an end to art. (*Joanne enters. Peter and Honey do not see her.*)

PETER

I think we've already put an end to art.

HONEY

Baby, we haven't even begun yet. (*Honey sees Joanne. Exits. Joanne is pacing around. Peter is watching either her or the floor. There is a long pause before there is any dialogue. There could be the start of sentences, but they never materialize into anything until*)

PETER

(*without animosity*) Fuck you. What's up.

JOANNE

Fuck you. Nothing much. (*silence*)

PETER

Come on, you've got something to say.

JOANNE

I wouldn't want to offend you.

PETER

I won't be offended.

JOANNE

It's . . I'm worried.

PETER

Well, don't be.

JOANNE

You don't tell me things anymore . .

PETER

Look . .

JOANNE

You always used to tell me things . .

PETER

Stop it. (*silence*) Is it Annie? It's not Annie, is it?

JOANNE

No.

PETER

Well then what?

JOANNE

You don't talk to anyone anymore.

PETER

That's the way it is. Look, I don't want to do this again. (*Peter moves to the piano — works something out. The silence is long.*)

JOANNE

When are you moving into the new house?

PETER

Maybe never.

JOANNE

What does that mean? Did you run out of money?

PETER

No. (*Bonnie enters.*)

CHILDREN OF THE KINGDOM

BONNIE

Peter, do you think you could come a little early tonight? There was such a problem with the lights last night and you're the only one . . (*sees Joanne*) I thought that you could . . I'll . . I'll talk to you later. Maybe you could just try to be on time tonight.

PETER

Okay. (*Bonnie exits.*) Look, Joanne, there are a lot of things on my mind . . a lot of things that I just can't put into words . . can't write down. Baby, if I could tell anyone . . It's not . . (*Annie enters.*)

ANNIE

Peter, Peter . . Some friends of mine are here from Kansas and they're just dying to meet you.

PETER

Kansas?

ANNIE

Yeah, they're really groovy. I've known them all my life and they came all the way out here to meet you.

PETER

Oh yeah?

ANNIE

Yeah. Let's go right now, okay? (*Peter and Annie exit. There is silence as Joanne, downcast, approaches Honey's drums. Honey has entered the studio, sees Joanne. She is not aware of his presence. Joanne, in a fury, strikes one of Honey's cymbals. Honey grabs her from behind.*)

HONEY

What's that?

JOANNE

Honey, I'm sorry.

HONEY

You want to play with the cymbals? Okay. We'll play. (*Feigns throwing the cymbal at her. Joanne is obviously afraid.*)

JOANNE

(*calling to the booth*) FLASH! (*There is no reply.*)

HONEY

Nobody home. (*Joanne attempts to leave but Honey intercepts her, grips her, and whispers something in her ear.*)

JOANNE

HONEY! (*Honey kisses her. Joanne exits, shaken. The band and the girls reenter the studio.*)

DAVID

Okay, girls. We're going to read that track. This time do it in unison. *(There is a short rehearsal of the girls' part of "Come On" with talk between the studio and the booth. As Peter enters the studio he looks things over and signals the beginning of the concert. As the song begins the lights change – the studio reality shifts to the concert.)*

ACE HANNAH with PETER

Come On

chorus:
Come along with me now.
I can make you,
reawake you,
I can shake you free.

Why don't you come and play.
I'll guarantee the fun —
no price too high to pay —
I just might be the one.
Your body knows the way
clouds open to the sun.

(chorus)

I'll take you to
places you've never seen.
Make you yield to
your own secret dreams.
Stay by my side,
come along for the ride.
Take a piece of me.
Eat and drink of me,
give yourself to me,
give yourself to me.

(chorus)

Tonight may be the night
that the angel fell.
Believe me, Mama,
I won't tell.
Move with me,
look into my eyes.
Too much delayed
and your dream dies.

CHILDREN OF THE KINGDOM

(chorus)

I'm the night rider,
come to my hotel room.
Let me be your cowboy there,
release you from your tomb.
Open wide to my message, Mama,
I want to plant my seed.
Don't be afraid to let me
give you what I know you need.

(chorus)

I see you start to smile
and I feel you changing seasons.
Come along with me.
It's taken you awhile
to see you don't need reasons.
Come along with me.
I need you
as much as you need me.
That's why I sing loud lullabies.

(chorus, repeated several times)

(As the song ends the band leaves the stage.)

OWENS

The band is going to take a short break . .

ACT TWO

Backstage or in a dressing room. All enter together.

GRANNY

Man, that was a workout.

JACK

Hey, did you hear the thing I did?

GRANNY

What was it?

JACK

Let's see . . maybe I can remember it . . down here somewhere. Oh, yeah.
Here it is. (*He plays it.*)

GRANNY

Yeah, yeah.

DAVID

He'll never remember it.

JACK

Sure I will, man. It'll just be a little different next time, that's all.

DAVID

You ought to write them down.

JACK

You know I can't read hardly at all.

DAVID

Somebody else could, though. "A Riff Composed by Jack Gordon" — how's that sound?

JACK

That's catchy.

HONEY

Stardom . .

JACK

"A Riff Composed by Jack Gordon" — sounds pretty good.

HONEY

It sounds lousy. (*to David*) Listen, if you really wanted to make some money you'd write down the drum parts.

DAVID

If you did it slow enough I'd do anything for you.

JACK

Did you see that chick up near the front? Man, she ate that shit up.

HONEY

We should have eaten her up.

DAVID

Now, now . .

JACK

"A Riff Composed by Jack Gordon" — I like it.

GREENE

(*to David*) Now look what you started.

DAVID

Well, he should write them down.

HONEY

There was one in a blue print dress with big tits.

GRANNY

I saw her.

JACK

I saw her. Man, what tits. We ought to invite them backstage.

CHILDREN OF THE KINGDOM

HONEY

The tits?

DAVID

We have enough problems as it is.

HONEY

They wouldn't be any problem. If they get out of line, you just let them have it.

JACK

The tits?

DAVID

There's enough chicks roaming around here as it is.

GRANNY

And most of them are fucking crazy.

HONEY

Crazy? (*Owens enters from the side door.*)

OWENS

Twenty minutes.

GRANNY

Hey, how was the gate on the last one?

OWENS

Better than we expected.

GRANNY

Commendable.

HONEY

Crazy. (*Owens exits.*)

GRANNY

(*to Peter*) What's the matter, man?

PETER

Nothing.

GRANNY

You're down about something.

PETER

I'm just thinking . .

GRANNY

Okay. Okay.

JACK

Hey, Peter, listen to this. (*He plays.*) Well what do you think?

PETER

I don't know, man.

JACK

Well, you've got to have an opinion. Do you like it or not?

PETER

I don't know right now.

JACK

Well, I thought we could use it sometime . .

PETER

Well?

JACK

Fuck, man.

DAVID

They weren't as worked up as usual.

JACK

They weren't out of their seats like always.

DAVID

A little bit — not like always.

HONEY

There was some old woman out there slowing the whole machine down.

GRANNY

It looked the same to me.

GREENE

You never look at the audience.

GRANNY

Sure I do.

PETER

Not too often.

GRANNY

Three weeks ago I did and you didn't even see me.

GREENE

Well, you don't. You might as well be playing in the studio.

JACK

You gotta put more class into it.

GRANNY

Fuck you and your class. I'm a musician, not a performer.

GREENE

We're performers more than we're musicians.

HONEY

They come to see us.

GRANNY

They come to HEAR us.

PETER

They come to see us . . haven't you learned that yet?

94

CHILDREN OF THE KINGDOM

GRANNY

Well, what the fuck is the matter with him? (*as Peter exits*)

HONEY

Lay back, man.

GRANNY

What the fuck is he doing?

JACK

He's tired, that's all.

GRANNY

Well, fuck him. We're all tired.

HONEY

That's enough, man.

GREENE

In another couple of weeks the tour will be over and then we can all cool off.

DAVID

A little time in the country would do us all some good. (*Owens sticks his head in the door.*)

OWENS

Fifteen minutes. (*exits*)

JACK

I'm ready to go. (*Jack starts to exit. Peter reenters.*)

PETER

I'm not doing the second show.

JACK

What?

PETER

I said, I'm not doing the second show.

GRANNY

Just what does that mean?

PETER

It means you do the second show without me.

GRANNY

No, man, it means you're fucking up.

JACK

Wait a minute . .

PETER

Well, whatever it means, you're on your own.

GRANNY

Oh, stop this shit.

DAVID
You really aren't going to do it?

PETER
That's right.

DAVID
Peter, come on . .

GRANNY
Fuck him. Jack'll sing.

JACK
Oh, no . . I'm not taking . .

PETER
Go ahead, Jack, sing.

JACK
I'd fuck it up.

DAVID
Are you angry about something we said? Something we did? We can talk about it . . (*Owens pushes his head in again.*)

OWENS
Come on, you guys, we've only got ten minutes.

GREENE
We're trying to take care of something here. (*Owens exits quickly.*) Peter, we're all tired.

PETER.
I know.

GREENE
It's silly for you not to do it. You'll only feel bad afterwards.

PETER
I already feel bad.

GREENE
You know why you're doing this, don't you?

PETER
No, I don't.

GREENE
It's the coke.

PETER
It's not the coke.

GREENE
Look, man, I don't think you even want to do this. (*Bonnie enters.*)

BONNIE
Say, that was a great set. (*pause*)

CHILDREN OF THE KINGDOM

JACK

(*to Bonnie*) See if you can do something.

BONNIE

What's the matter?

GRANNY

He says he's not doing the second show.

BONNIE

Why not?

GRANNY

Maybe it's a tantrum.

BONNIE

(*to Peter*) What's the matter, baby?

DAVID

Christ! I'll get Alan. (*exits*)

BONNIE

There's a big crowd out there, Peter. Lots of women. (*silence*) We've got great press coverage. Peter, we've worked hard to get where we are. Don't blow it now.

PETER

What do you want from me?

BONNIE

I don't want anything. I only want what's best for you.

PETER

What's best for me is not to sing anymore.

GRANNY

Horseshit, man. You're the one the press is coming to see. You're the one who has them coming and going — not us. It's a lousy kid's trick to leave us hung up like this. If you don't want to sing anymore, you can stop tomorrow, but not tonight — not while we're in the middle of something.

JACK

Man, what the hell are we gonna do?

GRANNY

You know what this is like? It's like the time in New York when we found Jack five minutes before showtime O.D.'d in the alley. And we canceled then, and that hurt us. But, Peter, he was dying . .

PETER

I'm dying, Granny.

GRANNY

What kind of a cocaine dream is that?

BONNIE

Maybe Michael can talk some sense into him.

97

PETER
I'm talking sense.

GRANNY
You're talking nonsense.

GREENE
Jack, see if you can find Michael. (*Jack exits. David enters with Weeks and Freddie.*)

WEEKS
(*to Bonnie*) What's the matter?

BONNIE
He says he won't go on.

WEEKS
Well, we'll see about that.

GRANNY
He won't listen to anything.

WEEKS
What's the matter, boy?

PETER
What do you want, Alan?

WEEKS
I don't want anything. I'm here to keep the contracts and keep you out of trouble.

PETER
You're doing a fine job.

GREENE
Peter, take it easy.

WEEKS
Is it money?

PETER
Get fucked.

WEEKS
I'm trying to find out what's the matter.

PETER
You're trying to fatten your wallet.

WEEKS
I'm doing that. So are you, by the way. You can sing. You need me to sell your voice.

PETER
And you think you don't need me?

WEEKS
That's not true. You're my top package.

CHILDREN OF THE KINGDOM

PETER

Your top package. That's really great. Tell me, Alan, who's going to be your top package when I'm gone?

WEEKS

What are you talking about?

PETER

You've already started thinking about someone else. Who is it? Who's going to be your top package when I'm gone, Alan? You don't give two shits about me.

GREENE

Peter . .

PETER

(*still to Weeks*) You don't give two shits about me. But you suck off what I produce. You don't care about anybody here. You just give us enough to keep going. (*to the band*) Don't you see that? He's the biggest asshole here.

WEEKS

Shut up. (*silence*) Now listen, we've got a contract. I'm responsible for seeing that the terms of that contract are carried out. The contract says you sing. That's how I sold it: for so much money, you sing. (*Jack enters with Michael.*) That's what I do, Peter, I buy things and then I sell them. I do it well, and I'm proud of it, so there's nothing you can say that's going to make me ashamed of what I am. You got that?

PETER

I sure do.

WEEKS

Now listen, a mistake here is going to fuck this whole band . .

PETER

Oh, Alan . .

WEEKS

All right. I know singing to a bunch of people really upsets you, Peter. But what else do you want to do?

PETER

I want to live.

WEEKS

When are you ever more alive? (*pause*) Now, if you don't go out there tonight, I'll be able to smooth it over, just like always. But the next time it won't be so easy. And the time after that I might not be able to smooth anything over. And then it'll get harder and harder for you to get bookings, and then you might just be through. So you'd better decide right here and now whether this little tantrum is all that important. (*pause*) Okay, Freddie, let's get some coffee. (*Weeks and Freddie exit.*)

DAVID

(*after Weeks*) Just a minute you mother fucker . . (*exits*)

JACK and GRANNY

Hey, David . . (*pause*)

GRANNY

(*to Peter*) I'm going out front to tune.

JACK

Me too. (*Granny, Jack, and Greene exit with Bonnie. This should leave the room empty except for Michael, Honey, and Peter.*)

PETER

(*to Honey*) What are you waiting for?

HONEY

I want to see what the big decision's going to be.

PETER

What do you think?

HONEY

I don't know. It depends on how much importance you place on what you're doing. Me, I'm just fucking around behind a set of drums. I don't give a shit for the audience, they don't give a shit for me.

PETER

Horseshit.

HONEY

But with you it's different. You've got the old fifty-fifty communication bit going. And that's what you've got to think about. That, and the guy on the motorcycle. (*Honey begins to leave.*)

PETER

Hey, where you going?

HONEY

To get some air.

PETER

But I haven't told you what I'm going to do.

HONEY

Well, when you decide you come out and tell me. I'll be waiting for you. (*Exits. Pause.*)

MICHAEL

Well, what was this one about?

PETER

I just don't want to do it anymore.

CHILDREN OF THE KINGDOM

MICHAEL

Well, do you know why?

PETER

Michael, do you think anyone understands what the hell I'm doing?

MICHAEL

Some of them do.

PETER

Yeah? Sometimes I think Weeks is the only one who has an inkling, and he's the last person in the world I want to know anything about me. I don't even know if you understand.

MICHAEL

Well, I'll certainly try.

PETER

Michael, it's getting to the point where I can go out there and jack off on the audience. I can tell them they're assholes, that their mothers are cunts. And they eat it up. I'm laying it down exactly like in a dream. I'm telling people off right to their faces, and they eat it up. You don't know what that does to my head. They eat it up and they scream for more.

MICHAEL

Well, why don't you tell me what it does to your head.

PETER

It isn't easy.

MICHAEL

Well, give it a try.

PETER

It has to do with a lot of things.

MICHAEL

I like B movies. I'm not going anywhere.

PETER

It's like the first time I was in that house I was going to buy. I could look down over the whole city, man — just a carpet of lights — and it was beautiful. And then someone says, that's downtown L.A. When was the last time you were in downtown L.A.?

MICHAEL

Yesterday. To score.

PETER

When you're above it, it's beautiful. But when you're down there, it's a dungheap. There're winos dead in the alleys, puking off curbs. Cats with one leg, or one arm, or no cock. The cops are downtown, man, running guys down in the streets. The jail's downtown. You ever been in jail, Michael?

(*Michael shakes his head.*) Well let me tell you — it's the bottom of the world. That makes downtown the suburb of the bottom of the world. That's why all the freaks live down there — they know they're going back to jail and they don't want to get too far from home.

MICHAEL

It seems to me that you'd want to get as far away as possible.

PETER

No, that isn't always true. Because when I was in jail I met some really fantastic people. That's where I met Honey. He's a weird mother fucker, there's no doubt about that, but I know that guy. You wouldn't believe some of the shit he's been into.

MICHAEL

Try me.

PETER

Anyway, I met some fantastic people down there. But I also met some assholes. Cats that fucked with me every single day I was there. Cats who roll old ladies. You got any idea how perverted you have to be to roll an old lady?

MICHAEL

Perverted — or desperate.

PETER

Either way, man. As much as I don't want to see the assholes again, there's a part of me that wants them around — that wants to be around them. That's why I've got Honey. He's a constant reminder of the bottom of the world. (*pause*) I'd like to be murdered by Honey.

MICHAEL

What?

PETER

I'd like to be murdered by Honey Carswell.

MICHAEL

Wait a minute . . I don't think I want to . .

PETER

I don't expect you to understand that.

MICHAEL

I don't think I want to understand it. Let's just try to figure out what you're saying.

PETER

I don't know. I only know that when I'm singing I'm way up there and I'm at the bottom. And there's truth on both ends, because I can feel it. The only thing is, I've got no control. Oh, I used to — maybe for the first few numbers, but after that I'm gone and something else takes over. It's like I was sitting out in the fucking audience listening to myself sing.

MICHAEL

And you want to quit?

PETER

Sure, man, it's killing me. It's to the point where I could fucking die on stage and I wouldn't even know it. I'd still be sitting in the audience listening to the music, watching my body go down and the chaos, and I wouldn't even care. I could fucking die out there and not even care. And the fucking audience pays to see that, and Weeks hustles his ass so that a whole lot of press and all those people will be here to see that. Everyone is just waiting for me to come out and rip open my flesh and bleed all over them, and they get a charge out of it, Michael. But they don't change. They don't change even when they see it, even when I'm standing out there bleeding to death. That's why I don't want to do it anymore. Not for those assholes. Not for people who come here and don't give a shit for what's really happening up here. There's nobody out there who's scared.

MICHAEL

Why should they be scared?

PETER

Why not, man? I'm scared. You're scared. (*pause*) I'm scared, Michael. (*pause*)

MICHAEL

You've been reading too much. Listen, Peter, it's only a matter of deciding what it is you want to do. We've always said we wanted to go eat drugs with the Indians. We could do that. Or if that's what you really want, we could get that house. (*stops, realizing that there's no escape for either of them*) Shit, I'm only trying to help you talk yourself into whatever the fuck it is you really want. (*long pause*) Look, Peter, I'm sorry I give such senile advice. But let's not overlook the fact that I score some supreme dope. Here. (*gives Peter some coke; stands, uneasy*) I think I'll go.

PETER

Hey, Michael, where are you going?

MICHAEL

(*exiting*) I'm sorry. (*Peter is alone in the room for a moment. Honey sticks his head in the door.*)

HONEY

Well, what's it going to be?

PETER

Be with you in a second.

HONEY

You're beautiful, man. (*Exits. Peter sits alone for a moment, then snorts or shoots the coke and exits. The band enters the stage for the concert, uneasy. Honey enters.*) He's coming. (*Peter enters and goes to the microphone.*)

ACE HANNAH with PETER

The Creeper

Creepin' at night
nowhere to go.
Stand in the alley,
long shiny hair.
Big sharp teeth,
blood in his eye.
He's never happy
'til he sees someone die.

chorus:
He's the Creeper.
He's the Creeper
and no child knows his name.

Layin' in bed
late at night.
You set the alarm,
turn out the light.
Feel a weight,
hear heavy breath.
Fingers reach out,
shake hands with death.

(chorus)

He never tells
just why he kills.
Some say he's hungry,
some say it's pills.
Sometime he come
stand in a crowd.
He might be out there,
look around now.
Feeling strange.
What can it be?

CHILDREN OF THE KINGDOM

Swear it's the Creeper
grinnin' at me.

(chorus)

Slow Freight Train

Standin' at the local depot
waitin' for the train to go
forty-two hours on the track,
I can hardly wait 'til I get back.
Slow freight train, baby,
hobo ride.
Slow freight train,
gonna climb inside.
She's been mean to me,
I know she's messin' round.
Slow freight train, baby,
back to my home town.

That woman's evil,
woman's just no good.
She's been treatin' me
like no woman should.
Slow freight train, baby,
hobo ride.
Slow freight train,
gonna climb inside.
She's been mean to me,
I know she's messin' round.
Slow freight train, baby,
back to my home town.

(At the end of the second verse Peter steps back from microphone, the lights dim, and we hear Toccata and Fugue in D Minor by Bach. Music is appropriate throughout the vision. Michael and Joanne enter from opposite sides of the stage and cross to Peter. Joanne is wearing wedding garb. Galadriel enters from the house and performs a mock wedding ceremony as Joanne and Michael place rings on Peter's fingers. As Peter kisses Joanne and then Michael the reporters enter from the house and take a flash picture of the ceremony. As the flash goes off the band freezes into grotesque postures behind Peter. Galadriel exits. Michael and Joanne cross behind Peter with gestures symbolic of their relationship with him, then move to opposite sides

of the stage. Weeks enters whistling, wearing a concessionaire's hat with a tray slung around his neck, removes a knife from the tray, and castrates Peter – slices – pauses. The girls realize what has happened and Weeks tosses portions to them, then exits through the house selling his product. The girls rush to Peter to comfort him, begin to assault him sexually, begin to fight among themselves, and pull to the sides of the stage still quarreling. The reporters begin to operate strobes as Bonnie appears behind Peter and the girls and laughs as a fun-house lady, tossing press clippings into the air while the band performs grotesquely and the organ plays circus music. The lights change and Alicia and Granny appear, pull Peter to his feet, and dance with him to idyllic music. The band freezes as Peter sees a masked figure of himself smiling. He approaches, the mask changes to a grotesque image of himself, then disappears, and he sees Honey mouthing the words "I love you" as Tommie approaches the microphone with Peter close behind and Honey threatening to attack Tommie. Blackout, Peter begins to sing in the dark.)

> I've been through this place,
> now there's nothing left to see.
> On your chain of lies
> I'm just a memory.
> And if your heart
> keeps on killing
> Then I will know
> the reason I died.

(As the song ends, Peter walks out of the concert. There is much confusion — Honey and Granny exit after Peter. Jack goes to the microphone.)

JACK

Peter's been taken ill, they tell me. We have a new singer, however. His name is Tommie, and we're going to do some kind of a blues. *(Tommie goes to the mike and introduces his song.)*

ACE HANNAH with TOMMIE

Welfare Song

> Welfare man calls it common law
> but you sure ain't common to me. *(repeat)*
> You were an expensive woman, baby,
> and now I got the fee.

(During this verse Honey and Granny have reentered and begun to play.)

> Daddy told me you got to hustle for the money
> but you know that ain't for me. *(repeat)*
> I'm going downtown and pick me some money
> from the welfare tree.

Gimme that pen and paper, baby,
let me sign on the dotted line. (*repeat*)
We're gonna be eating out tonight
drinking the expensive wine.

(*As the song ends the band and Tommie make a hurried exit at Bonnie's insistence. Owens enters.*)

OWENS

The concert has been canceled. We'll refund your money and let you know about a special concert when Peter's feeling better. (*Owens exits. The reporters rush onstage to question Bonnie as Weeks and Freddie enter.*)

BONNIE

I'm sorry, gentlemen, but both Peter and Mr. Weeks have already gone back to the hotel. (*Weeks and Freddie attempt to get out the side door but are intercepted.*)

NEWS I and II

Mr. Weeks! Mr. Weeks!

WEEKS

All right, gentlemen, I'm all yours. But one at a time.

NEWS I

What would cause Peter to walk off like that in front of an audience?

WEEKS

A slight case of the flu. He just wasn't satisfied with the job he was doing.

NEWS II

Did it have anything to do with drugs?

BONNIE

No!

WEEKS

Absolutely not.

NEWS II

Is there any truth to the rumor that he might be leaving the business?

WEEKS

He's never mentioned anything of the sort to me. As far as I know he's happy doing what he is doing. Peter's very concerned with the welfare of his audience. That's why he suggested doing a special show tomorrow night.

NEWS I

Whose idea was that?

WEEKS

Why, Peter's, of course. That's all I've got time for.

NEWS I

Just one more question.

WEEKS

All right. One.

NEWS I

What about this new singer that filled in for Peter?

WEEKS

Also Peter's idea. Now, if you'll excuse me . . Bonnie, would you take care of the press? (*Bonnie ushers them out amid questions. Owens enters.*)

OWENS

They're not happy out there.

WEEKS

I know, I know. Calm down.

OWENS

Calm down? I'm in hock up to my ears.

WEEKS

I know you are, Frank, and I'll take care of everything. You can go out there right now and tell them he's doing a special show tomorrow night. (*Granny enters.*) All right, where is he?

GRANNY

He's out in the alley.

WEEKS

What's he acting like?

GRANNY

He's pissed off.

WEEKS

Good.

GRANNY

Good? What do you mean, good?

WEEKS

Well, nothing makes him more pissed off than doing a bad show, right?

GRANNY

He's pissed off at you.

WEEKS

Yeah, well he'll get over it. Besides, he'll do a better show tomorrow night.

OWENS

A better show? Is that all you ever think about? A better show?

WEEKS

Why, Frank, I thought you were in hock up to your ears. That's what you want me to think about, isn't it? Look, that's all I've got time to think about — he's my job.

OWENS

And that's all?

WEEKS

That's enough. (*Owens exits through the house. Weeks turns to Granny.*) All right now, who's with him?

GRANNY

Greene's with him, Honey's with him, a couple of others. Alan, he's talking about being locked up in a black box . .

WEEKS

(*starts to exit, laughing on the line*) Jesus Christ . .

GRANNY

(*following him out*) What's so funny about that?

WEEKS

Not a goddamned thing, Granny. (*Freddie follows them out. The lights change to indicate an alleyway behind the auditorium. Granny and Weeks enter.*)

PETER

What do you want me to do, Alan?

HONEY

What are you asking him for?

PETER

Because he's the only one who can tell me.

HONEY

He doesn't know shit.

PETER

HONEY . . What do I do, Alan?

WEEKS

Well, it's all very simple, really. You just do a special performance tomorrow night. The press already knows about it. I told them you wanted to make it up to your fans. I told them that you wanted to give them the best show of your life, in order to make it up to them.

PETER

Where do I sign?

WEEKS

You don't have to sign anything.

PETER

I wish I didn't know you, Weeks.

WEEKS

No, you wish I didn't know YOU.

HONEY

What are you letting him talk to you like that for?

PETER

Because he's right.

109

HONEY

Right? He doesn't know shit.

WEEKS

Yes, right. I'm closer to him than you are.

HONEY

All right, asshole. Shove off.

PETER

Please . .

GRANNY

Honey, take it easy.

HONEY

Get out of here.

PETER

Listen . .

WEEKS

I'm just like a father to him. I'm a father to you, too.

GRANNY

Weeks! Stop it.

PETER

STOP IT! (*Honey hits Weeks. Peter starts to help Weeks up.*)

BONNIE

(*entering, to Greene*) What happened?

GREENE

I don't know. (*Honey hits Weeks again and is stopped by Peter.*)

PETER

HONEY!! (*Greene and Freddie help Weeks out.*)

BONNIE

I can't take this anymore.

PETER

Honey?

HONEY

What?

PETER

You all right?

HONEY

You gotta get rid of that guy. He's no damn good for any of us. Listen, don't do the show tomorrow night.

PETER

Honey, I've got to do it.

HONEY

For him? Yeah, you do it for him and see where it gets you.

CHILDREN OF THE KINGDOM

PETER

I'm not doing it for him.

BONNIE

I don't know. I just don't know.

HONEY

Son of a bitch is never satisfied.

PETER

Honey . .

HONEY

I'll kill that fucker if he comes in here again. (*Greene and Galadriel enter.*)

GREENE

(*to Peter*) Hey, let's not do that thing tomorrow.

GRANNY

What are you talking about?

GALADRIEL

Peter, Peter, I told you . .

PETER

Okay. Everybody shut up. (*They quiet down.*) Now, we're doing a show tomorrow night because I've agreed to it already. If we don't there'll be hassles following us around for months.

HONEY

So what? (*Annie, Madeline, and Pamela enter.*)

GREENE

Look, what kind of a show can we do?

GRANNY

I want to do this show.

GALADRIEL

Peter, don't do this show.

PETER

GALADRIEL — BE QUIET!!

GREENE

Look, man, there'll be other shows . .

PETER

Now wait just a minute . . I mean, I want to get rid of him now. Give him what he wants and get him out of here. Besides, we could use the money.

HONEY

Money? That's a bunch of shit. You're not doing it for the money.

PETER

I'm doing it for the money if I have to bail your ass out of jail for assaulting him. He'd do that.

111

HONEY

All right. I'll go talk to him about that right now. (*Granny restrains Honey.*)

GREENE

Hold it.

PETER

Stay here, man, stay here.

GREENE

What kind of show can we do?

PETER

GODDAMN IT — WE'RE DOING THE SHOW. And that's all there is to it. Shit. I'm gonna pay that fucker off and be rid of him. And that's all.

HONEY

Man . .

PETER

No, that's all. Everybody go back to the hotel — sleep it off. (*All exit except Honey, Joanne, and Peter. Honey exits. Slow fade-out.*)

ACT THREE

ACE HANNAH with PETER

Take Cover before Striking

Yesterday
just before supper
thought I'd take my ease.
Went down to the corner,
walked by the alley,
what do you think I see?
Young and old
they were clustered
round the garbage cans,
a congregation
for revolution
they reached out their hands.

chorus:
I heard them say,
let your words reflect your deeds.
Save the day
while there's still room to bleed.

No one smiled

and yet they wanted me
to come along.
Little boys with hand grenades
and one old man
with a Chinese gong.
What a bunch.
They'd figured all the ways
to win the war.
Dissolve the government,
the dues are fifty cents.
Could you ask for more?

(chorus)

I
didn't wait a minute,
jumped and joined the band.
Got a cache of guns
underneath my mattress
and I know the plan.
My eyes bug out
every time
I hear knocking at my door.
But don't call me paranoid.
I'm the son of Pretty Boy Floyd,
I'm a bad outlaw.

(chorus)

Still a Child

Our hearts are covered
with petals of smoke.
Peel back the layers to find
the cause of it all:
the spoon our songs are served on.
I come to you
but you meet me with a wall
too high for me to climb,
too far to fall.
I guess I'm still a child
who has not learned to crawl.

I came to you
in hope of a change,

113

open and willing to try
and rearrange
the way things ought to be.
Time and time again I've tried
but it's always just the same.
Before I get my bearings
I'm sucked into your game.
I don't want to hurt you
but there's no one left to blame.

I've been away
for far too long,
but now I have returned
to carry on
if you ask me to.
I come to you
but you meet me with a wall
too high for me to climb,
too far to fall.
I guess I'm still a child
who has not learned to crawl.

(Peter is shot during the singing of the last verse by an unknown audience member. Mass confusion. As this happens we hear over the loudspeakers the audience interviews from Act One and we see a documentary film of the killing.)

THE END

Children of the Kingdom by the Company Theatre Ensemble with script by Don Keith Opper was presented at the Company Theatre, Los Angeles, July 16, 1970–February 5, 1971. It was directed by Jack Rowe.

Cast of Characters

JASON	Dennis Redfield
FLASH	Donald Harris
TOMMIE	Don Keith Opper
JACK	Jack Rowe

CHILDREN OF THE KINGDOM

GRANNY	Robert Walter
FRANK OWENS	Michael Stefani
GALADRIEL	Sandra Morgan
GREENE	Wiley Rinaldi
PAMELA	Nancy Hickey
FORK	Ann Langston
DAVID	Steven Kent
MADELINE	Marcina Motter
BILL	Bill Dannevik
FREDDIE	Suzanne Benoit
JOANNE	Candace Laughlin
ALICIA	Nina Carozza
HONEY	Lance Larsen
BONNIE	Barbara Grover
MICHAEL	Michael Carlin Pierce
MARK MATTHEWS	Larry Hoffman
HARRY RANDALL	Richard Serpe
ALAN WEEKS	William Hunt
ANNIE	Trish Soodik
PETER	Gar Campbell

JOEL SCHWARTZ

Psalms of Two Davids

A PLAY IN TWO PARTS

for Danny, who was the source

Cast of Characters

SAMUEL, the prophet during Saul's reign, *who also plays*
NATHAN, the prophet during David's reign
SAUL, first king of Israel
JONATHAN, Saul's son, *who also plays*
ABSALOM, David's son
MICHAL, Jonathan's sister, *who also plays*
TAMAR, Absalom's sister
DAVID, as a youth in Saul's court
KING DAVID, a different actor from the young David
AMNON, David's firstborn son
All the remaining roles are played by a corps of actors

(NOTE. Although the play focuses on two periods during the life of David — one during the reign of Saul and the other during David's reign — the production should in no way suggest a biblical context.)

PSALMS OF TWO DAVIDS

PART ONE

THE REIGN OF SAUL

Prologue

SEER

There is no doubt among us:
the earth beneath us will
when least expected
quake.
Each day the prophets
with their matted hair
grow numerous and frenzied
in the crowded streets,
and a comet
in the form of a scuttlecrab
is sighted nightly
in the sign of the Scorpion.

It is said to refer to the king
Saul.

There are queues forming
at the mouths of caves
where witches
hold their counsel with the dead,
and the prophet Samuel
rends his·clothes
rolls his eyes

foams like a rabid dog
and curses
that he was made to inaugurate
over Israel
an age of kings.

No doubt, the earth will quake.

Scene 1

Bethlehem. The prophet Samuel is talking with Jesse and his sons.

JESSE
Samuel, what could you want with my sons?

SAMUEL
Send for David.

JESSE
Why him when there are my others?

SAMUEL
David.

JESSE
But he is a child.

SAMUEL
Let me see him.

JESSE
If I send for him he will shame me, for what does he know of talking to prophets? His life is a shepherd's life.

SAMUEL
Bring him here.

JESSE
Then say you will not take him from me. He was my last, and I knew he would be the last, and so I have a special fondness for him.

SAMUEL
Jesse. I have no time for this.

JESSE
Shammah. (*Shammah turns and David enters.*)

DAVID
Am I wanted?

JESSE
We have a visitor.

DAVID
Shammah told me.

PSALMS OF TWO DAVIDS

SAMUEL

David?

DAVID

Yes?

SAMUEL

You tend the sheep.

DAVID

Yes.

SAMUEL

Who is tending them now?

DAVID

My cousin.

SAMUEL

They say you write verses. Do you sing them?

DAVID

Yes.

SAMUEL

Will you stay a shepherd?

DAVID

I have no way of knowing.

SAMUEL

But you must have other dreams.

DAVID

Some.

SAMUEL

Of what?

DAVID

I have been seeing a great many stray sheep in the hills. They are not my father's, nor my neighbor's, but they need a mindful shepherd and they seem to have none. I find myself thinking beyond my father's flock, but these are just my daydreams.

SAMUEL

I think they are more than daydreams.

DAVID

(*about to protest, then changes his mind*) What's it like, God's voice?

SAMUEL

Have you never heard it?

DAVID

I feel He is just beyond my reach.

SAMUEL

Have you been expecting my visit?

DAVID

I cannot say.

SAMUEL

But you know now why I sent for you?

DAVID

My brother said, "Come." Nothing else.

SAMUEL

Yes . .

DAVID

He said you were here.

SAMUEL

I am here.

DAVID

That was all.

SAMUEL

The Lord spoke to me and said, "I will send you to Jesse the Bethlehemite, for I have provided Me a king among his sons." David, the time is come. (*David is stunned.*) I am taking you up to Gibeah, for there is need of a musician in the court of Saul.

DAVID

The king's court? King Saul? What would I do in the House of Kish? I am a shepherd!

SAMUEL

Come; we must go.

Scene 2

Saul's court. Saul enters and mimes dipping his fingers in a ritual laver. His behavior is erratic, but he makes an attempt at majesty.

SAUL

On the first dipping I wash my hands: spare me from the heaviness of my first dipping.

COURTIERS

Good day you, Saul, king of the Jews.

SAUL

I cleanse my soul, I purify my spirit, I wash my hands of my premonitions.

COURTIERS

God is with you, king of the Jews.

SAUL

On the third dipping . . on the second dipping . .

COURTIERS

(*severally*) If the House of Kish should ever sneeze . .

God bless . .

God bless . .

SAUL

Spare me, O Lord, from Your ruthless ways.

COURTIERS

God bless.

SAUL

Well now, as we have passed into the New Year — and safely, may I add, despite some of the witchy predictions — we are unharmed and victorious over our enemies to the north.

COURTIER

And they gifted us with the shell of a king. (*Saul laughs inappropriately.*)

SAUL

We are all now come to happier times. Why is it so dark? Is it evening already?

COURTIER

High noon.

SAUL

An eclipse?

COURTIER

High noon.

SAUL

I had not been told, and what is it supposed to mean?

COURTIERS

(*severally*) The shades are drawn . .

Leave it be cool . .

High noon . .

SAUL

And what do the astrologers say?

COURTIER

Too much and too little.

SAUL

Throw open the shades, I want the sun! Throw them open, wide!

COURTIERS

(*severally*) It will be hot, Saul . .

The sweat will run from your brow . .

From your armpits . .

Your crotch . .

Your feet . .

Saul . .

Saul, you don't want the sun . .

SAUL

Who are you to tell me what I want?

COURTIERS

(*severally*) Advisers . .

Friends . .

Kish sneezes . .

Bless . .

God save . .

God spare . .

SAUL

God spare? do you think so? Well, there's an interesting problem for my philosophers. Wrong! Philosophers! Magicians and necromancers, skittering about, huffing and puffing their magic formulas! Why, I have heard it said that Elijah himself in the form of a python — Bizarre, these goings-on. Has the world gone mad? Magicians . . wrong! I have heard it said — There's an interesting problem: in the form of a python — Elijah himself! — do you think so? Wrong! The world's gone mad, huffing and puffing and skittering about, bizarre! God spare these goings-on! I have heard it said — Wrong! wrong! wrong! wrong! Is it evening already? an eclipse? Wrong! wrong! Philosophers? advisers? friends? Where is my son Jonathan? Imagine, a python! Elijah himself! God spare! Did you know that rebellion is as the sin of witchcraft? Bizarre. But I have heard it said! Wrong! The world's gone mad! Well, there's an interesting problem: a world gone mad. There's one for the magicians and necromancers. Wrong! wrong! wrong!

COURTIERS

God save.

SAUL

On the first dipping . . Where was I? I am getting weary of this crown.

COURTIER

If the shell of a king sits on the throne, does he not wear the shell of a crown?

SAUL

He does, and it weighs like lead as he strains every inch of himself to feel it. (*Jonathan enters.*)

JONATHAN

You sent for me, Father?

124

PSALMS OF TWO DAVIDS

SAUL

The house is finally crumbling! At night I hear the rats in the walls, and I am told, "Look you, a household with rats is a house to be respected, the kitchens are full, the scraps are plenty." And at night, when I hear the rats scurrying with bits of food I repeat, "Respect! respect!"

JONATHAN

Father.

SAUL

Jonathan, I am only a pawn in the mind of a player I have never seen; chosen, not choosing, to make the opening moves, and for all I know the player of my pieces has been paid to throw the game. Will I be remembered as Israel's first and last king? For if I cannot pass the crown into your hands, a coven of witches will seize the throne! (*A courtier enters.*)

COURTIER

(*announcing*) The prophet Samuel has sent to you —

SAUL

We will not speak of Samuel!

COURTIER

— a player on the lute.

SAUL

I sent for no musicians.

COURTIER

But it will be, when the mood comes upon you, that he will play with his hand and you will be well.

SAUL

Who is the man?

COURTIER

His name is David.

SAUL

Then let him show me his face. Send him in! (*David enters, carrying his lute; all eyes are upon him.*) Will you stand there forever?

DAVID

(*bowing*) My lord?

SAUL

It seems you will be content to dazzle us with your looks.

DAVID

It is I who am dazzled.

125

SAUL

They tell me you sing. (*pause*) Sing! (*David, unsure of himself, begins to play his lute. During the song he notices Jonathan, whose eyes are fixed on him. Saul, his eyes closed, is soothed by the song.*)

DAVID

> Where is my warmth and comfort gone?
> What leaves me with this chill
> alone and mellow in the dark of the moon?
>
> Soft, my lord grows weary
> and his tranquil mind I fear is caught
> in tentacles of ill-borne thought;
> I pray him comfort in my tune.
> (O, will I see the loved one soon?)
>
> Touch me, hold me,
> make me golden
> in those eyes I've seen but once
> (and once is everything to me!)
> for surely in that face that sees me
> is my warmth and comfort gone!

(*The courtiers pick up the rhythm of the song on their drums and tambourines. Jonathan begins a mime-dance of swordplay and David joins him, to the courtiers' delight.*)

SAUL

(*his eyes still closed*) David?

COURTIER

I am here.

SAUL

You come from Judah?

ANOTHER COURTIER

Yes.

SAUL

You've come all the way from Judah to sing to me?

ANOTHER COURTIER

Do I please you?

SAUL

David . .

ANOTHER COURTIER

Yes?

SAUL

You will stay?

ANOTHER COURTIER

If my lord desires me.

SAUL

I will give you a chamber near my own, and when the evil mood comes over me, you will never be too far from me to play.

ANOTHER COURTIER

Nor from Jonathan! (*Saul looks up suspiciously.*)

Scene 3

A corridor in the court. Jonathan is walking down the corridor as Michal enters.

MICHAL

Jonathan!

JONATHAN

Have you seen David?

MICHAL

What, is this the new court greeting?

JONATHAN

We had plans to meet at sundown and I'm hours late.

MICHAL

So now you and I have this chance reunion after a week of absence — or shall I say neglect? — and do you say, "Dear sister, how I have missed you at my table"?

JONATHAN

Forgive me, but I must send word to him at once.

MICHAL

I should have guessed you must have David on your mind to see your composure so ruffled.

JONATHAN

Michal, do not mock me.

MICHAL

I speak, dear brother, out of nothing but jealousy.

JONATHAN

I know I have seen you too little these days, but that will be emended.

MICHAL

Jonathan, I am not so jealous of David taking my place at your table . .

JONATHAN

What then?

127

MICHAL

I am jealous that you can see him whenever you choose, that he talks to you, pours out his heart, looks in your eyes, all that; while the rest of us are queuing up for a chance to see him passing in the street.

JONATHAN

It does seem all the women are at his feet.

MICHAL

But I am not just a face in the crowd. After all, Saul is my father too, and in David's circles the name bears weight.

JONATHAN

Then we must all dine together soon.

MICHAL

I would love that, both for the chance to meet the Star of Bethlehem, and to be back at your table.

JONATHAN

I *have* missed you. And I've thought of an answer to last week's game.

MICHAL

But I won, I stumped you with "vintage."

JONATHAN

No, I never conceded.

MICHAL

Well?

JONATHAN

"Whilom."

MICHAL

Vintage to whilom . . Oh, that's very good. Perhaps I will reward you with some gossip.

JONATHAN

Shall we go to my house and talk over wine? I haven't yet eaten.

MICHAL

I would like that, but I'm late as it is. And besides, I'm sure David is waiting for you.

JONATHAN

What is the gist of this gossip?

MICHAL

In short, it seems our father is having second thoughts.

JONATHAN

About?

MICHAL

His lutist.

PSALMS OF TWO DAVIDS

JONATHAN

David?

MICHAL

It seems he is feeling possessive about the court's new jewel, and rather put out that David is not his to possess. Also, I hear he is growing jealous.

JONATHAN

Jealous of what?

MICHAL

The shepherd's charm. Surely you've noticed?

JONATHAN

But why should our father be jealous of someone more than twenty years younger than him?

MICHAL

Because, Jonathan, he is only now seeing that he has lost the ability to dazzle the court. (*David enters.*)

DAVID

Is this Michal?

JONATHAN

David! I didn't hear you coming.

MICHAL

(*eyes fixed on David*) Perhaps his feet never touched the ground.

JONATHAN

I'm truly sorry about being so late, but I had to review the archers and it was endless. I should have sent word.

DAVID

You need only have said Michal would join us.

JONATHAN

Unfortunately, she has other plans.

DAVID

(*to Michal*) Can they not be changed? I've been longing to touch the heart of Jonathan's sister.

MICHAL

(*lowering her eyes*) But I am afraid I cannot stay.

JONATHAN

We must all have dinner later this week.

DAVID

(*to Michal*) Send word that you are ill.

MICHAL

But you and Jonathan must have things to talk of.

DAVID

I want to be with both of you.

JONATHAN

David, you mustn't keep her. She's already late.

DAVID

Stay.

MICHAL

I could send word . .

DAVID

We'll find a runner.

JONATHAN

David.

DAVID

(*to Jonathan, admiringly*) She could only be the sister of my brother Jonathan.

JONATHAN

(*flustered*) We have always been close.

DAVID

(*to Michal*) Then it's been your good fortune.

MICHAL

(*also flustered*) You will make him blush.

JONATHAN

Must we all stand here when there is food at my house?

MICHAL

Do you truly think I should come?

DAVID

Please.

JONATHAN

It would be less awkward another night.

DAVID

For my sake, Jonathan, make her join us. (*Saul enters.*)

SAUL

What's this? As I see you together I think, ''Would that I were father to all three of these children.''

DAVID

My lord, if I may, I think of you as my second father.

SAUL

Then I will think of you as my second son. David, pull yourself away and play me a song on your famous lute.

DAVID

Oh! — I have something new for you. (*to Jonathan and Michal*) Forgive me, I had hoped we could have dinner and I shouldn't be pardoned for being so abrupt. But this is a song I've just composed and I'm eager to sing it for your father. Make plans for this week and I will surely join you. Please don't forget.

SAUL

Come, we will have wine and meat and music all night — a little feast for a shepherd and a king. (*David bows to Jonathan and Michal and joins Saul, who is quite pleased with himself for winning David away.*)

Scene 4

Ramah. In the distance a chant is heard, continuing into the scene.

CHANT

Saul the migh-ty (*beat*) sol-dier

has slaugh-tered (*beat*) his thou-sands (*beat*)

but Da-vid (*beat*) of *Beth*-le-hem

has slain ten thou-sand (*beat*) sol-diers . .

(*Lights come up on Samuel deep in meditation. David approaches and kneels, sitting on his heels. Samuel comes out of his trance. He has been trying to summon David psychically; David knows this, for he feels summoned.*)

DAVID

You wanted me.

SAMUEL

Your visit is overdue.

DAVID

I've been kept busy.

SAMUEL

By the court life?

DAVID

It's been turning me around.

SAMUEL

There is something about the manner of a Judean shepherd that has the power of magic in a Benjamite court.

DAVID

I have not understood these attentions.

SAMUEL

How do you find Saul?

DAVID

I love him as my father.

SAMUEL

And Jonathan as your brother.

131

DAVID

Yes.

SAMUEL

All Israel sings of you and Jonathan.

DAVID

I know.

SAMUEL

And with your own verses as well.

DAVID

I have been told to write songs.

SAMUEL

Beware of Saul.

DAVID

He has asked me —

SAMUEL

David, you walk through the streets; surely you are not deaf to the women's chanting.

DAVID

Oh, they are always at the gates of the city.

SAMUEL

Then surely Saul has heard them.

DAVID

He knows I am not the hero they sing of. I have never fought a battle in my life, yet they make up victories for me.

SAMUEL

But they sing and believe it, and this he knows. And the Lord is with you. This too he knows. Saul may still wear the crown, but in truth the kingdom is no longer his. David, Saul is afraid of you.

DAVID

He would never think anything ill of me.

SAMUEL

Saul is unfit to be king in Israel; the time is ripe for the crown to change hands.

DAVID

I think you are wrong.

SAMUEL

The kingdom is yours for the asking. (*pause*)

DAVID

I am not asking.

SAMUEL

I am asking.

PSALMS OF TWO DAVIDS

DAVID

How can you mean this? Samuel, I am a shepherd and a lutist — not a king.

SAMUEL

A king is not needed; I made that mistake once. What the people truly need is a shepherd to lead them.

DAVID

But I am young and out of place in the court as it is!

SAMUEL

You have made the court yours.

DAVID

Samuel, how could you think I'd go against Saul? Usurp the throne? I love him as my father!

SAMUEL

As a king he is unfit. David —

DAVID

No!

SAMUEL

The time is come.

DAVID

I will not rise up and take the throne! Samuel, you are a prophet of God; how can you ask me to defy His chosen king?

SAMUEL

The Lord is no longer with Saul.

DAVID

But, Samuel, my heart *is*!

SAMUEL

Do you now serve your heart at the expense of the Lord?

DAVID

I cannot believe it is meant for me to cut Saul down while he lives and breathes.

SAMUEL

It is God's will.

DAVID

No!

SAMUEL

I see now that you have not heard His voice.

DAVID

My heart tells me what I do is right, and how can this not be God's will? It is Saul's kingdom, the Lord chose him, and I have only your word that it is time for me to be king.

133

SAMUEL

Then give me your hand and look at me. (*David, uncertain, takes Samuel's hand and stares into his eyes.*) If the Lord has faith you will do His will, let Him make His will known to His stubborn servant. For it does you no good to think that I might be a mistaken prophet. (*In the distance the chant is heard again.*)

CHANT

Saul the mighty soldier
has slaughtered his thousands
but David of Bethlehem
has slain ten thousand soldiers . .

Scene 5

Afternoon.

DAVID

Jonathan!

JONATHAN

I knew you would be here.

DAVID

Where are you coming from?

JONATHAN

I had dinner with Michal.

DAVID

Is she well?

JONATHAN

Yes, she's in very good form.

DAVID

She made honeycake.

JONATHAN

How do you know?

DAVID

The look on your face, like a spoiled twelve-year-old.

JONATHAN

Does it really show? You know, she can't stop talking about you.

DAVID

But we've only spoken to each other once.

JONATHAN

To her dismay.

PSALMS OF TWO DAVIDS

DAVID

You're mocking me.

JONATHAN

No, I mean it. Really, when Michal talks of you her eyes go all fiery and she gets very womanish.

DAVID

And you encourage her.

JONATHAN

I like to hear you talked about.

DAVID

But it makes me feel like the harlot of Gibeah.

JONATHAN

Come now, the court's never been so full of life. And my father is pleased.

DAVID

Even with our friendship?

JONATHAN

He wants it so.

DAVID

Wants, or wanted?

JONATHAN

What makes you suddenly so suspicious?

DAVID

Am I being suspicious?

JONATHAN

Have you been to see Samuel?

DAVID

I've owed him a visit.

JONATHAN

Then that's what it is. You mustn't let my father know.

DAVID

Of course I won't.

JONATHAN

What do you see in him?

DAVID

Samuel?

JONATHAN

He's wrecked my father's life.

DAVID

Don't be foolish.

JONATHAN

Oh sure, he's been a great friend, hasn't he?

DAVID

He made your father king of Israel.

JONATHAN

Only to regret it.

DAVID

Regret?

JONATHAN

Well, what else is it if not petty jealousy?

DAVID

It's just that Saul has not been well.

JONATHAN

He's been victimized, David.

DAVID

We shouldn't talk of this.

JONATHAN

(*a bit too casually*) You don't really love him, do you?

DAVID

Jonathan, I do!

JONATHAN

Then why do you hurt him?

DAVID

Hurt him? How?

JONATHAN

Since you've arrived the women sing only praises of you. It used to be him. I mean, before the moods.

DAVID

But what have I to do with the women?

JONATHAN

Couldn't you write a song about Saul?

DAVID

I do — constantly! — but they change the words to make me the hero.

JONATHAN

Then write about the battle of Yabesh-Gilead, when he was still the people's hero and the Lion of Benjamin.

DAVID

I should never have left the hills of Judah.

JONATHAN

But you've made Gibeah a place of love. My father depends on you, the court is indebted to you, my sister lives to get a glimpse of you, the people crowd the streets in hope of seeing you. And I need you.

PSALMS OF TWO DAVIDS

DAVID

So many people cannot depend on me.

JONATHAN

They love you.

DAVID

They will slay me with their love. I'm so afraid of being held.

JONATHAN

No one is holding you.

DAVID

Except for you.

JONATHAN

Are you afraid of me?

DAVID

Not of you, but of me. I don't know what I would do if God's will set me against you.

JONATHAN

How could that be?

DAVID

I hope I don't destroy you.

JONATHAN

You couldn't.

DAVID

I could.

JONATHAN

Please, David, there is no good to be had in this indulgence.

DAVID

Jonathan, never forget that my soul will always be knit with yours.

JONATHAN

Never . . even when I am king. (*The realization that Jonathan will never be king, and that this is something he must never know, halts David.*) David, what is it?

DAVID

What?

JONATHAN

Your thought.

DAVID

I heard God's voice.

JONATHAN

(*suspending disbelief*) What was it like?

DAVID

Cold.

JONATHAN
What did it say?
DAVID
It babbled.

Scene 6

Saul's room. In the distance the chant is heard again.

CHANT
Saul the mighty soldier
has slaughtered his thousands
but David of Bethlehem
has slain ten thousand soldiers . .
(*Lights come up on Saul, alone, but speaking as if with confidants.*)
SAUL

Where are they all, now, doing what, at this minute? Let me think, they must be catalogued, I must not misplace them lest they rise up against me, thinking I neglect. (*half-aware of the fading chant*) What are they shouting? I can hardly think. So, to our lists. It may be wise to watch the ministers of state, or those with aspirations. Ha, an endless start right there, it would be a full career just naming them all. I'd have to lie in wait all day . . to lie in wait, prepared . . after all I cannot tell what plots they have devised for my beheading . . I will have spears! I will have the court manned with carriers! Unless . . of course! — among *them* lurks the enemy, waiting for me to say, "Fill the court! surround me!" Well, do I not remember how to throw a spear myself? I need a deadly weapon, a goodly one, forged of the finest and sharp! — to be kept at my side always so I can hurl it deftly at the first suspicion. Saul henceforth shall not be seen unarmed! . . (*As Saul continues, two spear carriers enter in stylized movement to the beat of the chant. They step high, poise themselves, step broadly with spears in hand, take a stance, step and thrust, retrieve the lunge and start again, making their way across the stage unaware of Saul.*) But what of those moments when I must show trust? Show or feign, whatever. As with Jonathan perhaps. Where is he now, have I left him out of my listings? He would not be in his room at this hour — What is the hour? Or maybe he is with David, though I think not, no, he must be with Michal, and she is laughing at his stories, yes, he is making her laugh. And she asks of me, what does she ask? She asks, "Do you think he is well?" And he says — what does Jonathan say? — I am well? would he truly defend me? Well, so much for Jonathan. And David . . Of course, *he* could be with Jonathan, but what would Michal be doing then? Why must I go through these details? Of all the court these three are surely with me. Or two at the least. Weird, how David is more my child than Michal . . (*to the spear carriers, halting them*) Hold! I said I would have spears, give me one to keep at my side, a spear for the king! But off, get out, I will not have a bodyguard of strangers; do you think I am blind to your scheming dances? (*Takes a spear as the spear carriers resume their stylized movement. As they exit, the chant fades completely.*) See, they are quiet now, they've stopped their endless babbling at the gates. There are no heroes left to sing of. (*calls out*) David! Come, play me a song and spend an evening by my side! (*David enters with his lute.*)

DAVID

Did you call me?

SAUL

David, do you love me?

DAVID

Were you my first father I could not love you more.

SAUL

Do you love Jesse?

DAVID

I love him deeply.

SAUL

Good.

DAVID

You should not doubt my love.

SAUL

My only doubts are those of one who loves too much and fears it cannot all be returned.

DAVID

My lord, I too have such doubts.

SAUL

Then sing for me.

DAVID

Is the mood upon you?

SAUL

No, thank God, I am feeling well, and I would have some comfort if it is not too much to demand of you.

DAVID

I am only too happy to please you.

SAUL

Then sing, I long to hear your voice.

DAVID

> I went up to the hills and looked over Galilee
> and lifted my eyes unto the Lord;
> "What of the heroes who fought here?" I cried,
> "Where are the men who won peace for these hills?"
>
> And my voice went out to the Sea of Galilee,
> to the mountains of Dan and to Yabesh-Gilead,
> seeking the names of the mighty warriors
> who gambled their blood for Israel's sake.
>
> And my voice returned from the Sea of Galilee,
> came rushing down from the mountains of Dan,
> and from Yabesh-Gilead the echo called,
> "Praise the Lion of Benjamin whose name is Saul."
>
> I lifted my eyes to give thanks to the Lord
> and I filled myself with the tranquil sounds,
> and for all I saw of an Israel I cherished
> the name of Saul was emblazoned on my heart.

SAUL

(*suddenly in a fit of anger*) Do you take me for a fool?

DAVID

What have I said?

SAUL

Tell me, is David truly thinking of Saul?

DAVID

Is my song so unclear?

SAUL

Unclear? Not at all. But *too* clear!

DAVID

I can't understand you.

SAUL

Do you think I have not heard your other songs? the praises to David's glory they sing at the gates? Do you think I am so stupid as to be pacified by this new drivel of yours?

DAVID

But my lord —

SAUL

Be careful now.

DAVID

Those other songs —

140

SAUL

Be careful, David, I am wiser than you think.

DAVID

They are not my songs!

SAUL

Oh, then you expect me to believe the women prefer to sing the songs of secondary poets?

DAVID

But you misunderstand!

SAUL

David, I do not care who wrote those songs.

DAVID

Then why do you blame me?

SAUL

For thinking that I am a fool!

DAVID

But I don't!

SAUL

Yet you sing me my praises and play dumb to the fact that I am everywhere else ignored because of you?

DAVID

It is not my fault!

SAUL

Whose fault is it then? If David had not been born, they would not sing of David!

DAVID

Do you wish me dead?

SAUL

If David had not been born — !

DAVID

Then I too wish myself dead!

SAUL

Granted! (*He thrusts the spear, but stops short of piercing David.*)

DAVID

(*after a moment*) Do you truly wish this? (*Saul's mood changes; he begins to laugh.*) My lord?

SAUL

Do you not see that I merely jest?

DAVID

Truly?

SAUL

Could I harm you?

DAVID

I don't know.

SAUL

David, I was testing your love.

DAVID

Testing?

SAUL

My child, I could no more do you harm than I could fall on my spear.

DAVID

You confuse me.

SAUL

You are young.

DAVID

I am not as young as I was in Judah; I am growing older here in the court.

SAUL

(*reaches for David*) David — Do not flinch, I am not going to beat you.

DAVID

Have I done you any wrong?

SAUL

The joke is over, laugh, it is done. I have other things to speak of.

DAVID

Perhaps you are tired and would rather rest.

SAUL

Quiet! I said the joke is over! Do not tax me with your childish tedium! (*relaxes*) There are more important things. David, do you truly feel you are growing older?

DAVID

Yes, and quickly at times.

SAUL

Then it is not too soon to speak of marriage.

DAVID

Marriage!

SAUL

Surely a man must think of marriage.

DAVID

I have never given it any thought.

SAUL

You are being modest, no doubt, what with all the women falling at your feet wherever you go.

DAVID

I think you mock me.

SAUL

Only because your eyes are fixed on the stars and you haven't looked down to see the women swooning. But I have been thinking of a wife for you. Do you trust me as your father?

DAVID

I have said so.

SAUL

Then what do you say to my daughter?

DAVID

Michal?

SAUL

Surely she is comely and spirited.

DAVID

But who am I, and what is my life, or my father's family in Israel, that I should be son-in-law to the king?

SAUL

I have always thought of you as my son; and then Jonathan will truly be your brother.

DAVID

My lord —

SAUL

Well look, we will say no more on it. Go off and think, and when you are ready you will tell me your answer.

DAVID

If that is your wish, I — (*Suddenly Saul grabs the spear and seems about to lunge at David, who is caught off balance. But Saul laughs, and David looks at him uncertainly. As David exits, he sees Samuel in the shadows watching him.*)

SAMUEL

The kingdom is yours. God's will!

Scene 7

The wedding. There is a procession with music to Michal's house; an empty litter is carried. At Michal's house, Saul hands Michal over to the group and she sits on the litter. As she is lifted up David appears by her. Lights focus on David and Michal as all others freeze.

DAVID

The moment has come.

MICHAL

David.

DAVID

Are you happy?

MICHAL

Look at them all, so envious of me.

DAVID

Because of me?

MICHAL

Of course, because of you.

DAVID

And envious of me, because of you.

MICHAL

What a pair we make.

DAVID

Do you think so?

MICHAL

No one will henceforth know what either of us is really like.

DAVID

Is that what you want?

MICHAL

Completely! (*David withdraws and the procession continues. Mimes and dancers lead the way as Michal is carried to the temple. Jonathan leads a smaller procession as David enters, wearing a garland of flowers. The first procession cries out.*)

PROCESSION

Here is the bridegroom! (*Lights focus on David and Michal as all others freeze.*)

DAVID

I won't confide in Jonathan anymore.

MICHAL

But you will.

DAVID

Not if you don't want me to.

MICHAL

I want you to be happy, even — David, we will be married within the month.

DAVID

I know, the contract is settled.

PSALMS OF TWO DAVIDS

MICHAL

Can you see what we will be like as man and wife?

DAVID

Devoted completely to one another.

MICHAL

Don't lie, David, admit what it will be, so I will prepare myself not to want more.

DAVID

Can you be content with only half of my heart?

MICHAL

No, not if I am your wife, but it will be worse without you.

DAVID

I am bound to others.

MICHAL

David, you'll always be thinking of Jonathan, won't you?

DAVID

I'm trying to think of you. (*The wedding resumes. David takes Michal off the litter and they stand before Jonathan, stage center.*)

JONATHAN

"Look toward heaven and number the stars if you can, and so shall your descendants be." (*The celebrants shower the couple with confetti as one speaks.*)

CELEBRANT

And the bride and the bridegroom
were showered by the court
with the wheat of the harvest
and gold of the treasury,
and they turned to leave.
(*The lights focus on David and Michal as all others freeze.*)

DAVID

(*brisk and cheerful*) Michal, it's David.

MICHAL

You've finally come.

DAVID

I know you've been hinting.

MICHAL

My brother was faithful.

DAVID

Faithful?

MICHAL

To me; for once to me . . Do you feel very powerful?

DAVID

Because of the court's attention.

MICHAL

No; because of my attention.

DAVID

Michal, you make me feel humble.

MICHAL

I think you are playing with me.

DAVID

But the game is yours.

MICHAL

How did you know? (*The wedding resumes with the simultaneous lighting of candles for all the celebrants to carry on a recession from the temple to David's house. As the couple withdraws, the lights focus on them at right and Jonathan at center as all others freeze.*)

JONATHAN

You know, she can't stop talking about you.

DAVID

But we've only spoken to each other once.

JONATHAN

To her dismay.

DAVID

You're mocking me.

JONATHAN

No, I mean it. Really, when Michal talks of you her eyes go all fiery and she gets very womanish.

DAVID

And you encourage her.

JONATHAN

I like to hear you talked about.

DAVID

(*to Michal*) I've been longing to touch the heart of Jonathan's sister.

MICHAL

(*lowering her eyes*) But I am afraid I cannot stay.

DAVID

(*to Jonathan, admiringly*) She could only be the sister of my brother Jonathan.

JONATHAN

(*flustered*) We have always been close. (*The wedding celebration resumes and is concluded as the stage clears of everyone but Saul and Jonathan.*)

146

SAUL

Jonathan . .

JONATHAN

Father?

SAUL

Now we have her in his house, so that we may ensnare him, and David will no more be a thorn in my side. (*exits and leaves Jonathan alone to realize the loyalties he is suddenly torn between*)

Scene 8

The roof of David's house. David is singing with his lute.

DAVID

The law of the Lord is perfect,

reviving the soul;

the testimony of the Lord is sure,

making wise the simple;

the precepts of the Lord are right,

rejoicing the heart . .

(*During the following verse, lights come up at random on soldiers, singly and in pairs, doing the spear-carrier dance.*)

The commandment of the Lord is pure,

enlightening the eyes;

the fear of the Lord is clean,

enduring for ever;

the ordinances of the Lord are true,

and righteous altogether.

More to be desired are they than gold,

even much fine gold;

sweeter also than honey and drippings of the honeycomb.

(*During the following verse, lights come up on Jonathan and Michal. They look at each other, their actions strained, and he makes a formal bow. Lights fade on them.*)

Moreover by them is Your servant warned;

but who can discern his errors?

Clear me from my hidden faults.

Keep back Your servant from presumptuous sins;

let them not have dominion over me!

Then I shall be blameless,

and innocent of great transgression.

(*Jonathan enters.*)

JONATHAN

Do I disturb my brother-in-law?

DAVID

I was singing.

JONATHAN

Am I welcome in your presence?

DAVID

Jonathan, why this constrained tone?

JONATHAN

Absence.

DAVID

Since the marriage? (*Jonathan nods.*) But not distance.

JONATHAN

Truly?

DAVID

Do you think my heart can have changed?

JONATHAN

David, is all well with you?

DAVID

Everything. Except that I have missed you.

JONATHAN

I have received no invitations.

DAVID

Invitations? When were invitations ever necessary?

JONATHAN

They have become necessary.

DAVID

Please, Jonathan, do not act as if anything has changed.

JONATHAN

Is my sister well?

DAVID

You've seen her.

JONATHAN

Once, but we said nothing. I didn't know what to say.

DAVID

That's unlike you.

JONATHAN

Yes, I know, I'm quite polished in court. But this is not the court.

DAVID

It is my home.

PSALMS OF TWO DAVIDS

JONATHAN

I know.

DAVID

And yours. Jonathan, we are now brothers in name as well as in spirit. We should be closer.

JONATHAN

It's difficult.

DAVID

You'll always be the master of my heart.

JONATHAN

And you of mine. David, I am caught between two sides.

DAVID

But I count on your strength.

JONATHAN

There are times I fear I am not in control.

DAVID

It's an illusion anyway, the feeling of control.

JONATHAN

Perhaps, but a comforting illusion. David, I worry about you here.

DAVID

For what reason?

JONATHAN

Saul.

DAVID

But we are at peace. He's made me his son.

JONATHAN

Not out of love, David; or rather, too much out of love for him to live with.

DAVID

How so?

JONATHAN

He plans to use Michal against you.

DAVID

Michal?

JONATHAN

Thus the marriage.

DAVID

Are you sure?

JONATHAN

I am sure.

DAVID

Does she know?

JONATHAN

I doubt it.

DAVID

Do not worry, she would not help him.

JONATHAN

But her defiance will only spur him on even more. He doesn't trust her as it is.

DAVID

Jonathan, what are you trying to tell me?

JONATHAN

Saul will not rest while you live.

DAVID

Truly?

JONATHAN

In his own words.

DAVID

Spoken in a fit?

JONATHAN

And spoken in lucid times as well. Even today. David, it hurts me to betray him, but you must protect yourself.

DAVID

How?

JONATHAN

You must hide.

DAVID

Hide?

JONATHAN

His men will seek you in this house. It is all that's on his mind.

DAVID

But hide for how long? Forever?

JONATHAN

Listen. Take heed to yourself in the morning, stay in a secret place and hide yourself, and I will speak to my father about you. If I learn anything I will tell you.

DAVID

Do you mean this?

JONATHAN

It's what I came to say, even uninvited. I didn't know if you would receive me as a neglected brother or an estranged one, but I came to warn you out of the love I will always have for you. David, heed my words.

DAVID

(*thinks for a moment*) I will be in the caves near Hebron.

JONATHAN

Within the week I will come. And don't let anyone know, not even Michal. Tell her you are off to Bethlehem, or better yet to Ramah to see Samuel. She will know to keep that secret.

DAVID

All right.

JONATHAN

You will go, won't you?

DAVID

If you think it so important. You know I trust you.

JONATHAN

My heart is with you.

Scene 9

Saul's court. Saul and Jonathan are alone drinking.

SAUL

I have only two years left in me, Jonathan, not much more than that. You're not afraid, are you?

JONATHAN

Just . . not ready.

SAUL

I have no doubts, you'll make a fine king. A better one than your father.

JONATHAN

Not so.

SAUL

Modesty. Which is not a family trait. God knows I don't have it, and your sister is not overly endowed with the virtue. (*pause*)

JONATHAN

I don't see her much anymore.

SAUL

Truly, daughters grow up and leave their fathers, and their brothers also are left behind. Do you think she is happy?

JONATHAN

I'm sure she is.

SAUL

I'm not. I don't think anyone can be happy with David.

JONATHAN

Why do you say that?

SAUL

Because he is slippery. One moment he is yours, but only for a moment, and you don't know you've lost him until you find yourself fighting to win him back. Surely you've noticed.

JONATHAN

I have not seen that side of him.

SAUL

Oh you, you'd defend him to your death. All his little tricks have sucked you in.

JONATHAN

He plays no tricks with me.

SAUL

You don't see them, but he's devious, he manipulates everyone.

JONATHAN

How can you fault him? He sings your praises, he glorifies the court —

SAUL

He spins a net and ensnares us all because we are too busy being dazzled to see what he is doing.

JONATHAN

What ill has he done?

SAUL

Don't you see how he is playing at subterfuge, acting the part of my beloved friend while seducing the court away from me? Jonathan, I fear he will fight you for the crown.

JONATHAN

He would never fight me.

SAUL

Not now, there's no point to fight you now, but when the time comes you will see your friend in a new light.

JONATHAN

These suspicions are false.

SAUL

I have thirty years on you: do you think I have wasted those decades?

JONATHAN

I didn't say that.

SAUL

Then trust me, listen to me, I know.

PSALMS OF TWO DAVIDS

JONATHAN

I don't.

SAUL

Take my word. Jonathan, my only dreams are wrapped up in you. As for myself, I have somehow bungled things along the way, and I regret that the kingdom I leave you is in a shaky state. But I take solace in the knowledge that I tried. Believe me, I did try my best, and if I failed it was because I couldn't see the outcome of actions I took. But for all that has happened, I know I risked all I had and I take pride in knowing that. I was just no match for a silent God who concealed His will.

JONATHAN

You haven't failed.

SAUL

Jonathan, let us not pretend to each other.

JONATHAN

Israel is whole, and look around you: the court has never glittered so before.

SAUL

You can only see David wherever you look.

JONATHAN

I didn't even mention David.

SAUL

In what other way does the court glitter?

JONATHAN

Trust me, father, he loves you, he honors you, he's devoted to you.

SAUL

To my destruction.

JONATHAN

You insist on being deaf to anything I say in his favor.

SAUL

Only as you are deaf to me.

JONATHAN

And are you planning his destruction?

SAUL

Just as he is planning mine.

JONATHAN

Why will you sin against innocent blood by killing David without cause?

SAUL

Oh Jonathan, you will persist in this till the end, won't you?

JONATHAN

Answer me.

SAUL

I am much too weary to fight you. (*closes his eyes*) As the Lord lives, he shall not be put to death. (*A light comes up on David, but only Jonathan sees him.*)

DAVID

What is my sin before your father that he seeks my life?

JONATHAN

Far from it! You shall not die.

DAVID

Are you certain of this?

JONATHAN

My father does nothing either great or small without telling me, and why should my father hide this from me? It is not so.

DAVID

Your father knows well that I have found favor in your eyes, and he thinks, "Let not Jonathan know this, lest he be grieved." But truly, as the Lord lives and as your soul lives, there is but a step between me and death.

JONATHAN

Whatever you say, I will do for you.

SAUL

(*opening his eyes and seeing David as if in a vision*) I am much too weary to fight you. But Jonathan, are you truly with me? I have no other friend. (*He begins to tremble, sensing a mood coming on.*)

Scene 10

The roof of David's house. In the dark the chant is heard.

CHANT

Saul the (*beat, beat*) soldier (*beat*)
has slaughtered (*beat, beat*) thousands (*beat*)
but David (*beat, beat*) David (*beat, beat*)
tens (*beat*) of (*beat*) thousands . .
(*The chant fades as lights come up on David, singing with his lute.*)

DAVID

           The heavens are telling of the glory of God,
           and the work of His hand is revealed in the earth;
           day to day pours forth speech,
           and night to night declares knowledge.
           There is no speech, nor are there words;

their voice is not heard;
yet their sound goes out through all the earth,
and their words to the end of the world.

(*Michal enters.*)

MICHAL

Do I disturb my husband?

DAVID

I was singing.

MICHAL

David, I worry about you here.

DAVID

For what reason?

MICHAL

Saul.

DAVID

But we are at peace.

MICHAL

David, if you do not save yourself tonight, tomorrow you will be killed.

DAVID

What have you heard?

MICHAL

His soldiers are coming, and you'll be slain with lute in hand.

DAVID

Are you sure?

MICHAL

Saul will not rest while you live.

DAVID

Then I shall be forever running, for I will not raise my hand against him.

MICHAL

Go now, I will help you. David, I could go with you, I would spend my
life running with you, but I will stay for now because I can be most useful
to you by dealing with Saul.

DAVID

Michal, these times will surely pass, and we will yet receive happiness
from the Lord.

MICHAL

Hurry, and God save you.

DAVID

Take the lute. (*She lets him down behind the roof as two soldiers rush
in and take hold of her.*)

155

MICHAL

Let go of me!

FIRST SOLDIER

Where is your husband?

MICHAL

What do you want with him?

SECOND SOLDIER

We were sent to fetch him and bring him to the king.

MICHAL

He is sick.

FIRST SOLDIER

Where is David?

MICHAL

He is sick! and in bed! let him be! (*Saul appears.*)

SAUL

Why do you deceive me thus, and let my enemy go, that he is escaped?

MICHAL

He said to me, "Let me go, why should I bring death to both of us?"

SAUL

You wretched child! Have the times so changed that the husband's word outweighs the father's? (*Jonathan is brought in by two soldiers.*)

MICHAL

Jonathan!

SAUL

Where is he?

JONATHAN

I don't know.

SAUL

Surely you have been told where he has fled!

JONATHAN

I don't know!

SAUL

Don't lie to me!

JONATHAN

I am not lying!

SAUL

Thou son of perverse rebellion! don't I know that you have chosen the son of Jesse to your own shame, and to the shame of your mother's nakedness? For as long as the son of Jesse lives upon the earth, you will not be established, nor your kingdom! Now send and fetch him to me so that he should be counted among the dead!

PSALMS OF TWO DAVIDS

JONATHAN

Father —

SAUL

We will pursue him, and seek him out, and cut him down! And you, Jonathan, you will lead the troops! Hush, not a word, lest you make me mad! (*to the soldiers*) Let them go. (*Saul and the soldiers exit.*)

MICHAL

Jonathan . .

JONATHAN

Tell me: what shall I do?

MICHAL

You cannot go to war against David.

JONATHAN

But neither can I defy Saul.

MICHAL

He is wrong!

JONATHAN

He's my father!

MICHAL

You fool — he's mad!

JONATHAN

Not mad but defeated and deserted! Michal, who in all Israel stands behind him? I know his soldiers and they bow to the crown, but what do they care of the man who wears it? Michal, he was a hero in his prime! he was singled out to establish a kingdom!

MICHAL

But look at him now! He is no more a king than a hero.

JONATHAN

Wrong! — he is still the king, and also our father!

MICHAL

And when he says kill, you kill? Jonathan, how can you turn your heart against David?

JONATHAN

My heart is more with him now than ever.

MICHAL

Then stop this battle!

JONATHAN

You heard him, he spoke, and how can I defy his will?

MICHAL

But how could you possibly lead his troops?

JONATHAN

Because when we march into battle my father will look to see if I am there,
and if I am not it will kill him.

MICHAL

So you will make this battle?

JONATHAN

For Saul's sake, yes.

MICHAL

And for David's sake?

JONATHAN

For David's sake I will not bear arms.

MICHAL

You will surely be slain!

JONATHAN

That well may be. But if I bear arms it is more than likely that I will
come back with my brother's blood on my hands.

MICHAL

Then promise me this: you will give no orders to do him harm.

JONATHAN

Upon my heart, I could not bring myself to hurt David.

MICHAL

Jonathan, you will be fighting both sides.

JONATHAN

I will surely lose.

MICHAL

Yes, but also you will surely win.

JONATHAN

Either way you will lose one of us.

MICHAL

Don't! (*The drums of battle are heard.*)

Scene 11

*The battle between David and Saul. The drums are heard again. Silence.
Then drums and trumpets, as the lights come up. Three actors, holding
open libretti, read the following in concert fashion.*

FIRST ACTOR

Sau-l (*drum*) the migh-ty (*drum*) (*drum*)

SECOND ACTOR

Sau-l   the

PSALMS OF TWO DAVIDS

THIRD ACTOR
Sau-l

FIRST ACTOR
Saul the (*drum*) the (*drum*)   the
SECOND ACTOR
Saul the   the   the
THIRD ACTOR
                    the mad!

FIRST ACTOR
migh-ty (*drum*)   (*drum*) (*drum*)
SECOND ACTOR
migh-ty
THIRD ACTOR
            but *Da*-vid

FIRST ACTOR
Saul the migh-ty sol-dier
SECOND ACTOR
        Saul the sol-dier
THIRD ACTOR
                Da-vid

FIRST ACTOR
has slaugh-tered   his   thou-sands
SECOND ACTOR
        has slaugh-tered   thou-   sands
THIRD ACTOR
            slain   ten   thou- sands!

(*A soldier appears up left doing the spear-carrier dance; two more enter down right doing the dance. When the three meet at center, the second and third lunge; the first stiffens, pivots, falls backward into their hands and is dragged off. During the following, several actors creep up around the edges of the stage.*)

FIRST ACTOR
Saul the (*drum*) the (*drum*)   the
SECOND ACTOR
Saul the   the   the
THIRD ACTOR
        Da-   vid   *Da*-vid

159

FIRST ACTOR

migh-ty (*drum*)   (*drum*) (*drum*)

SECOND ACTOR

migh-ty

THIRD ACTOR

  has slain ten thou-sands!

(*David enters furtively and approaches a group of actors.*)

DAVID

I have a favor to ask of the priests of Nob.

PRIEST

Why are you alone, and no man with you?

DAVID

The king has sent me on secret business that no one else can do for him.

PRIEST

And what is the favor?

DAVID

Some loaves, for I was sent in haste.

PRIEST

Here, and God be with you. (*David withdraws to the far side of the stage and crouches to eat the bread unseen.*)

FIRST ACTOR

Saul the migh-ty   (*drum*)

SECOND ACTOR

    Saul the

THIRD ACTOR

      Da-vid

FIRST ACTOR

the (*drum*) the migh-ty   the (*drum*)

SECOND ACTOR

the   the migh-ty   the

THIRD ACTOR

  Saul   the mad king!

(*They put down the libretti and join the other actors as trumpets sound. Saul enters, carried on the shoulders of two soldiers.*)

SAUL

Hear me, you Benjamites! will the son of Jesse give you fields and vineyards? will he make you captains of thousands, and captains of hundreds of thousands that you have conspired against me? Why did none of you tell me when

160

my son made a league with the son of Jesse? is there none of you at all that is sorry for me, who would tell me that my son turned my servant against me, to lie in wait this very day? Let me hear the priests of Nob, who gave loaves to my enemy.

PRIEST

Who among us is so trusted as David, and who is as honorable in the family of Saul?

SAUL

You will surely die! you and all of this house! Slay the priests of the Lord, for their hand is with David! fall upon them all! (*As actors at random cry out and fall, slaughtered, David speaks.*)

DAVID

(*to himself*) I have done this and brought about their death! They were guiltless, all of them, and their blood is on my hands! What have I done that this should happen?

SAUL

(*to soldiers around the stage*) Go and find where David is hiding! (*The search begins, with stylized movement and a percussion background.*)

SOLDIER

(*seeing David*) He is found in the cave of Adullam! (*David flees.*)

DAVID

Be gracious unto me, O God, be gracious unto me,
for in You my soul takes refuge;
yea, in the shadow of Your wings will I take refuge
till the storms of destruction pass!

SAUL

Where is David?

ANOTHER SOLDIER

(*seeing David*) Hiding, in the land of Moab! (*David flees.*)

DAVID

For strangers are risen up against me,
and ruthless men seek after my life;
they do not set God before them!

SAUL

Where is David?

ANOTHER SOLDIER

(*seeing David*) Hiding, in the forest of Hereth! (*David flees. During the following, Jonathan enters in search of David, but trying to remain unseen.*)

DAVID

My heart does writhe within me
and the terrors of death are fallen upon me.

Fear and trembling come upon me
and horror has overwhelmed me!

SAUL

Find out who has seen him, for he deals most subtly. Tell me, where is
David?

ANOTHER SOLDIER

(*seeing David*) Hiding, in the city of Keilah! (*David flees, and Jonathan
catches his sleeve.*)

JONATHAN

Don't be afraid, for the hand of my father will not find you, David.

DAVID

Jonathan!

JONATHAN

Hear me: it is you who will be the next king of Israel, and I shall be there
by your side!

DAVID

The Lord be between me and you!

JONATHAN

Between my seed and your seed!

DAVID

Forever!

JONATHAN

I must go! (*He does not move, but David flees.*)

SAUL

Go see, and take knowledge of all the places where he hides! Where is
David?

ANOTHER SOLDIER

(*seeing David*) Hiding, in the wilderness of Ziph! (*David flees.*)

DAVID

My soul is among lions,
and I lie among them that are aflame!

SAUL

Where!

ANOTHER SOLDIER

(*seeing David*) In the hill of Hachilah! (*David flees.*)

DAVID

O that I had wings like a dove!
I would fly away and be at rest;
yea, I would then wander afar,
I would lodge in the wilderness;

PSALMS OF TWO DAVIDS

I would haste me to a shelter
from the raging wind and tempest!

SAUL

Where!

ANOTHER SOLDIER

(*seeing David*) In the wilderness of Maon! (*David flees.*)

DAVID

O Lord, how many are my foes!
Many are rising up against me;
many are saying of me,
there is no help for him in God!
O Lord, how many are my foes!

ANOTHER SOLDIER

He is here in the caves of En-gedi!

SAUL

Stop, I am weary, let us rest for the night. (*The soldiers lower him. To one of them he speaks.*) Come, and stand guard at the mouth of this cave, that I may go in and sleep for a while. We will find him in the morning. (*Saul lies down with his spear beside him, unaware that David is behind him and watching.*)

DAVID

(*to the actors who have not been pursuing him*) Who will go down with me to Saul's camp?

ABISHAI

I will go down with you. (*The two creep up behind Saul, unnoticed.*) God has delivered your enemy into your hand. Now let me kill him, I pray you, with the spear to the earth at one stroke, David, and I will not strike him a second time.

DAVID

Don't touch him, let him sleep; we already have too much blood on our hands.

ABISHAI

But he will surely kill us when he awakes. Let me go, David, please.

DAVID

No, stay, but quiet, not a sound! (*Soft drums. David crawls forward, takes Saul's spear, and retreats with Abishai. Loudly he calls out.*) Can the guard of the king of Israel hear me? (*Saul wakes and, finding his spear gone, freezes in terror.*)

GUARD

Who calls?

163

DAVID

I have heard that you are known for your service to the king!

GUARD

What do you want?

DAVID

Why is it, then, that you kept a poor watch? For during this night someone came unto the king and nearly did him harm. Surely it was not good of you to let this thing happen. As the Lord lives, you deserve to die! And now see who guards the king's spear!

SAUL

Is this your voice, my son David?

DAVID

It is my voice, my beloved king. Why does my lord pursue his servant? for what have I done? or what evil is in my hand? I pray you, do not let my blood fall to the earth!

SAUL

Return, I will do you no more harm, David, for my life was precious in your eyes. I have played the fool, and made a great mistake.

DAVID

Let one of your men come fetch your spear. (*Jonathan rises and receives the spear from David. Impulsively, they embrace, and Saul is broken by the sight.*)

SAUL

O Jonathan, my son, my son! fetch the spear and let us go! (*The drums begin to roll and gradually recede.*)

Scene 12

Ramah. Samuel is sitting tailor-fashion, and David is kneeling in front of him.

DAVID

Samuel, what will become of us all?

SAMUEL

When you are ready you will know.

DAVID

But now, believe me, I feel blind and I want to see. I've caused much pain, and I don't know why; I'm caught in a net, and I can't get free; I've made myself a burden to the king, and I used to be salve to his wounds. Now I make them fester.

PSALMS OF TWO DAVIDS

SAMUEL

You were warned.

DAVID

But I told you then I could not understand God's will if it was that I be king.

SAMUEL

And have you learned?

DAVID

I have only learned that the most unlikely turns of fate are the only ones that happen. There is no way of counting on anything human.

SAMUEL

Do you trust the Lord?

DAVID

With all my heart. But now I'm lost. What has He revealed to you that shows the sense in what is happening?

SAMUEL

David, He only gives me a glimpse of the order in what seems random; but I do not pretend to understand the logic of that order piece by piece.

DAVID

I tried my best to be mindful, but look what has happened. Why? Samuel, I see only chaos!

SAMUEL

What do you want?

DAVID

To see the point!

SAMUEL

Are you asking me for a handful of wisdom?

DAVID

Just give me knowledge! Show me the outcome, show me the order, show me that the pieces fit so I don't give up!

SAMUEL

The knowledge will make it more difficult, but give me your hand and look at me. These are the things that will happen, David, but by then I will be gone. (*David takes his hand and looks in his eyes. In another part of the stage Jonathan enters, pursued by four soldiers from the previous scene. As they corner him, Saul enters and freezes to see one of the soldiers thrust his spear into Jonathan. Saul, beyond grief, rushes to the soldier, takes his spear, falls upon it, and collapses with Jonathan, dead. The soldiers withdraw. David, his heart breaking, pulls away from Samuel and climbs to the highest point on the stage.*)

165

JOEL SCHWARTZ

DAVID

O Israel, your glory is slain on high!
How are the mighty fallen!
(*In the distance, a dirge is heard.*)
Saul and Jonathan, beloved and lovely!
In life and in death they were not divided;
they were swifter than eagles,
they were stronger than lions!
How are the mighty fallen in the midst of battle!
I am grieved for you, my brother Jonathan;
a comfort have you been to me,
and your love to me was wonderful,
passing even the love of women.
O, how are the mighty fallen!
(*Slowly the cast gathers around the edges of the stage, and as the lights dim they chant the Jewish prayer for the dead. David gradually joins them, trying to lose himself in ritual, but he is overwhelmed by a feeling of meaninglessness.*)

MOURNERS

Yitgadal v'yitkadash sh'meh raba
be-olma dibera ki-re-uteh v'yamlik malkuteh
be-hay yekon u-beyo mekon u-behay-ye dekol bet Yisrael
ba-agala u-bizman karib
   v'yimru Amen.

Yitbarak v'yishtabah v'yitpa-ar v'yitromam
v'yitnas-se v'yit-hadar v'yitaleh v'yit-halal
sh'meh dekudsha berik Hu
le-ela u-le-ela min kol birkata v'shirata
tush-behata v'nehemata da-amiran ah! be-olma
ah! ah! ah! ah! ah!
   v'yimru Amen.

PART TWO

THE REIGN OF DAVID

Prologue

Saul, son of Kish,
son of Aviel, son of Ts'ror,
son of Bechorat,
son of Aphiach of the tribe of Benjamin,
king of Israel:
yitgadal v'yitkadash
    v'yimru Amen.
Jonathan, son of Saul,
son of Kish, son of Aviel,
son of Ts'ror, son of Bechorat,
son of Aphiach of the tribe of Benjamin:
yitgadal v'yitkadash
    v'yimru Amen.

O Israel, your glory is slain on high!
how are the mighty fallen!

Samuel, son of Elkanah,
son of Yerocham,
son of Elihu,
son of Tohu,
son of Tsuph of the tribe of Ephraim,
prophet:
yitgadal v'yitkadash
    v'yimru Amen.
SEER
The earth did quake
and those who lived
recount it as a legend
and a half-forgotten tale
designed
to excite
young children.
And the prophets
with their matted hair

say again the earth will quake —
for when the same disaster
comes a second time
then someone will
surely
take heed.

Scene 1

Near the court. Amnon and Absalom are engaged in swordplay as Tamar sits watching them.

ABSALOM

This doesn't seem to be your forte.

AMNON

Perhaps if something were at stake.

ABSALOM

Your honor is not sufficient?

AMNON

Absalom, my honor is not in question.

ABSALOM

Then what stakes would you suggest? Silver?

AMNON

Something more worth fighting over.

ABSALOM

Then I suggest my sister Tamar. (*sensing her reaction*) What's that bristling I hear?

AMNON

Our sister if you please.

ABSALOM

Ours, Amnon? We have no mother in common.

AMNON

But a common father.

ABSALOM

Oh, I would not call David common.

AMNON

In common, if you will.

ABSALOM

I wonder what he would say, the king being called common by his own son.

PSALMS OF TWO DAVIDS

AMNON

And I suppose you'll try to find out.

ABSALOM

Me? For what reason?

AMNON

You'd invent one.

ABSALOM

Would I?

AMNON

It is well known that Absalom has reasons for everything he does.

ABSALOM

Is it.

AMNON

And the motive is usually Absalom, at that.

ABSALOM

Well! It seems I am being provoked. And what do they say of Amnon: that he is selfless?

AMNON

They say very little.

ABSALOM

Why is that, I wonder?

AMNON

They are all too busy speaking of Absalom.

ABSALOM

Well, I confess I do command more attention.

AMNON

Gossip.

TAMAR

Attention.

ABSALOM

You see? Tamar has spoken.

TAMAR

I thought you both had forgotten me, and here I was sitting — the spoils waiting to be carried off by the victor.

AMNON

Then, Tamar, do you agree to our terms?

TAMAR

Of course I agree. I have always been partial to valiant men.

ABSALOM

And as you may have noticed, she has only been seen with me of late.

AMNON

Subject to change.

ABSALOM

Truly?

AMNON

Women love power, and Absalom, you forget —

ABSALOM

I do not forget.

AMNON

— though I lack your charm, and certain skills —

ABSALOM

Are we bringing up tedious subjects, brother?

AMNON

Oh, so I am "brother" now! full brother, not the half-brother you prefer to call me. Does my claim to the throne mean so much to you?

ABSALOM

Not nearly what it means to you. In chronology, Amnon, you are first, number one; but by all other standards —

TAMAR

Absalom, let's not be children. What would Israel think to hear this quibbling in David's household?

ABSALOM

Our well-tempered father may have much of the Balance in him, but he cannot keep us from doing a little tipping here and there.

AMNON

To the point, Absalom. Are we wagering over Tamar's favor or aren't we?

ABSALOM

I must say, this is the greatest show of stamina I have seen in you yet.

AMNON

When the price is right . .

TAMAR

The price! Hold now, I will not be called chattel. Are we speaking of a woman's dowry or of my favor?

AMNON

No offense was meant.

ABSALOM

(lunging) As offense goes, you're a disaster.

AMNON

Very clever. (They freeze.)

PSALMS OF TWO DAVIDS

KING DAVID

(*entering*) Lord, when I was a child I thought beyond my father's flock and sought to be a mindful shepherd. I remember Your voice was just beyond my reach. Since then I have taken a great many stray sheep and made them into one flock. But in leading my own sheep, Father, am I wanting? (*The sons bow.*)

TAMAR

Father.

DAVID

Continue, please, I have come to be entertained by my children.

AMNON

As it is, we were nearly finished.

DAVID

Truly?

AMNON

If you'll excuse me, I am a bit short of breath.

DAVID

Then pause awhile and I will send for some wine.

AMNON

If it pleases my father, I would rather retire to my room.

DAVID

It would please me more to have you stay. But if you are tired . .

AMNON

Exceedingly.

DAVID

Then go and have some rest. (*Amnon bows to the three and exits.*) I haven't seen the three of you together since the Passover, and that is now many weeks past. I told you, Tamar, how comely you were then, and now you are even lovelier. Is it the spring?

TAMAR

I am always happiest this time of year.

DAVID

It pleases me beyond words to have you sparkle so among my children. And not just among my children, but among all the children of Jerusalem. Even of my wives and concubines, there is none that has captured the heart of this city as you have. They say that Tamar sets the fashions by what she wears.

TAMAR

Am I blushing, Father?

ABSALOM

You — blushing? She lives on this talk.

DAVID

It seems you do compete with her in turning heads.

ABSALOM

Do I?

DAVID

Such an innocent look! It's a good thing I said it first, else you would have wasted no time in pointing it out to me.

ABSALOM

Compete is the wrong word; we travel as a team.

DAVID

And soon they'll be saying, "King David — isn't he the father of that famous pair, Absalom and Tamar?"

TAMAR

Do I detect a note of jealousy?

DAVID

Child, I too had my day turning heads. But tell me, why did Amnon withdraw so quickly?

ABSALOM

I think he is unused to the sword and tired himself out.

DAVID

Is that all, then?

ABSALOM

I think so.

DAVID

No quarrel between you?

ABSALOM

Only the wit of two quick brothers.

DAVID

You're incorrigible. Come now, take a walk with me, I want to see how Jerusalem looks in its first spring as the City of David.

TAMAR

Father, you're blushing.

DAVID

It's pride, and I seem not to wear it as easily as my children do.

TAMAR

Will you forgive me for not joining you?

DAVID

Must you go?

PSALMS OF TWO DAVIDS

TAMAR

I have promised to bake with the women.

DAVID

Then you may go only if you promise there will be treats at my table tonight.

TAMAR

A promise.

DAVID

(*kissing her*) My blessings go with you.

ABSALOM

You will have dinner at my house?

TAMAR

If I am expected.

ABSALOM

As usual. (*She nods, bows to David, and exits.*)

DAVID

You take all your meals together?

ABSALOM

Nearly all, except when we are at your table.

DAVID

Your friendship, you know, is sung throughout Israel.

ABSALOM

Our father had such a friendship once.

DAVID

Yes; they are rare. (*The two begin to climb a high platform.*)

ABSALOM

Your silence . .

DAVID

What?

ABSALOM

Have I stirred memories?

DAVID

Pleasant ones.

ABSALOM

I was afraid that perhaps —

DAVID

No, I am not saddened. I cherish those days. He would have loved Jerusalem.

ABSALOM

The city is growing beautiful. They even speak of it in Damascus, so I have heard.

DAVID

I have such a love for these hills. Look, Absalom, look around on all sides, it's like a precious stone, Jerusalem. Over there, Absalom, look, they're planting olive trees, and there are oranges. O Absalom, I have not felt so peaceful since I was a child in Bethlehem.

ABSALOM

Nor have I seen you so happy.

DAVID

There is yet one thing I dream of for Jerusalem. It is a fine city now, and will be great one day, but not until it has become a resting place for God. I have been dreaming of the Holy Ark; it has never come to rest, after years of being carried through the wilderness of Sinai, into a forgotten homeland, with no more shelter than a shabby tent set up here and there along the way. And where does it rest now but in the hands of some Judean priest for safekeeping. It should be brought to Jerusalem, Absalom; imagine the day, with the timbrel and psalter and all the young girls dancing in linen and playing the tambourine. And only then, when the Ark is at rest, will Jerusalem transcend being David's City and truly become a City of God.

ABSALOM

As you speak of it I see it.

DAVID

Then we will make it happen.

ABSALOM

Father, how do I say . . how does the son of David say he loves his father?

DAVID

O Absalom, my son!

ABSALOM

I . . I must go back to the city. Will you give me leave?

DAVID

Go with my blessings. (*Absalom bows and exits. As David looks after him, and over Jerusalem, a soft rhythm begins to build. David bursts out.*)
The earth is the Lord's and the fullness thereof!
the world and they that dwell therein!
For He has founded it upon the seas,
and established it upon the floods.
Who shall ascend into the hill of the Lord?
and who shall stand in His holy place?
He that has clean hands and a pure heart;
who has not lifted up his soul unto vanity

nor sworn deceitfully.
He shall receive the blessing of the Lord
and righteousness from the God of his salvation.
Such is the generation that seek Him,
that seek Your face, O God of Jacob!
(*cymbals*)

Scene 2

Absalom's house. Tamar and Absalom have just finished dinner and are playing a word game.

ABSALOM

Cruet?

TAMAR

Cruet.

ABSALOM

(*thinks, then emphatically*) Vintage.

TAMAR

Oh, that's very good.

ABSALOM

Go on. Vintage. (*brief pause, then a rapid volley*)

TAMAR

Whilom.

ABSALOM

Sage.

TAMAR

Tamarind! (*They laugh, appreciating what has been a clever choice on Tamar's part.*)

ABSALOM

All right, I concede, you win, Tamar.

TAMAR

That makes it three this evening.

ABSALOM

I guess I'm no match for you.

TAMAR

On the contrary, Absalom, you always set me up perfectly.

ABSALOM

Then as long as I'm doing something perfectly, I needn't win as well.

TAMAR

Whatever Absalom does he does perfectly.

ABSALOM

Truly?

TAMAR

They say he acquired that skill from his sister.

ABSALOM

Do they?

TAMAR

Oh, don't ask me, I never listen.

ABSALOM

Lies, lies.

TAMAR

Indeed, if I did, I might grow vain.

ABSALOM

For shame.

TAMAR

Enough of this. Tell me, why did Amnon leave so quickly after father came in?

ABSALOM

I think — he is ashamed.

TAMAR

Ashamed?

ABSALOM

To be our father's first, and to be his heir, and to be so far beneath him in stature.

TAMAR

But surely David does not slight him.

ABSALOM

No, he has been more than just in distributing his favors. When we are alone together, father and I, talking of this or that, I can see the gleam in his eye that says I am favored. But when we are not alone he leans over backward toward his firstborn son, lest Amnon suspect and grow jealous.

TAMAR

But you say, nevertheless, he is ashamed.

ABSALOM

Sister, though David cannot be faulted, surely Amnon is not blind to the fact that he falls so far short of David's standards. Amnon is not dull, I don't mean that, but he is not quick either. He sees very little beyond his immediate range, and I fear he will make a poor king in his day. But these are not my matters, he will most likely be king, David will choose him for the sake of his birthright, and I cannot quarrel with one who weighs issues as carefully as our father.

PSALMS OF TWO DAVIDS

TAMAR

Then I will give it no more thought.

ABSALOM

What troubles you, Tamar?

TAMAR

Nothing; you've reassured me.

ABSALOM

Come now, what is it?

TAMAR

A look, nothing more.

ABSALOM

From David?

TAMAR

From Amnon.

ABSALOM

All right, what kind of look?

TAMAR

I catch him gazing at me out of the corner of his eye as if . . it's hard to say precisely . . My love for you strikes him as a choice I've made between the two of you.

ABSALOM

But we are not your only brothers.

TAMAR

Nevertheless. And my choosing you is proof to him of all you have that he lacks. I don't know why he values my preferences so highly. But this look, it's as if he felt he would become you if I chose to sit at his table nightly.

ABSALOM

Well, this must be some look!

TAMAR

Don't mock me.

ABSALOM

Forgive me, but I think you are just being womanish.

TAMAR

You're a beast.

ABSALOM

Indeed? Well, tell that to my brother.

TAMAR

You're horrid.

ABSALOM

But if I may quote my sister, *all* my qualities are acquired from Tamar.

177

TAMAR

That only applies to the virtues.

ABSALOM

I see. (*pause*) Sulking?

TAMAR

No.

ABSALOM

Then what?

TAMAR

Oh! I have something to show you.

ABSALOM

The subject is being changed?

TAMAR

Was there more to be said?

ABSALOM

No, I think not, you have had the last word.

TAMAR

Then I'll show you a new dance.

ABSALOM

A dance? What brings that up?

TAMAR

I just remembered.

ABSALOM

Impossible to keep up with you.

TAMAR

Let me show you, Absalom. It's the dance I will do when father brings the Ark into Jerusalem.

ABSALOM

And if Tamar dances a new dance, all Jerusalem will follow. Let me see how it is done. (*A tambourine is heard as Tamar rises and begins to execute some graceful steps. Behind her the stage is cleared of the table and props. Two women enter and dance with Tamar, as the scene shifts to the streets of Jerusalem. The music builds as an exultant procession fills the stage. Slowly a canopied cart bearing the Ark is wheeled on, followed by a joyful King David. As the growing rhythms of the tambourines, harps, and cymbals surge through him, he bursts into a dance of celebration. When the Ark is at center, the dancers and celebrants gradually exit in all directions; and the prophet Nathan is carried in, sitting tailor-fashion on a litter. He is lowered, facing David, with the Ark between them.*)

178

PSALMS OF TWO DAVIDS

DAVID

Nathan! see now, I dwell in a house of cedar, but the Ark of God dwells only within curtains.

NATHAN

Thus says the Lord, "Shall you build Me a house for Me to dwell in? for I have not dwelt in a house since the day that I brought up the children of Israel out of Egypt, even to this day, but have walked in a tent and in a tabernacle. In all the places wherein I have walked, spoke I a word with any tribe saying: Why have you not built Me a house of cedar? Thus says the Lord unto David: I took you from the sheep that you should be prince over My people Israel, and I have been with you wheresoever you did go. And I will make you a great name, and your seed after you, and your throne shall be established forever."

DAVID

Who am I, O Lord God, and what is my house that You have brought me thus far? There is none like You, nor is there any God beside You, according to all that we have heard with our ears! O Lord of hosts, the God of Israel, has promised this good thing unto Your servant; let it please You to bless the house of David forever! O Lord! my Shepherd!

VOICES

. . I shall not want.
He makes me lie down in green pastures;
He leads me beside the still water;
He restores my soul;
He leads me in the paths of righteousness for His name's sake.
Yea, though I walk through the valley of the shadow of death,
I fear no evil, for You are with me;
Your rod and Your staff, they comfort me.
You prepare a table before me in the presence of my enemies;
You have anointed my head with oil; my cup runs over.
Surely goodness and mercy shall follow me all the days of my life,
and I shall dwell in the house of the Lord —

VOICE

(*cries out*) Behold! He that keeps Israel neither slumbers nor sleeps! (*drumroll, which repeats and grows ominous*)

Scene 3

Amnon's room. Amnon is with his servant. Down left, in a dimly lit area not part of the room, is David; left of center, in a dimly lit area, is Tamar;

179

and up right, dimly lit, is Absalom. These three are not part of the scene
at first and stand immobile.

SERVANT

My lord Amnon, why are you growing leaner from day to day?

AMNON

Can I trust you?

SERVANT

You have always done so.

AMNON

Then hear me, Yonadav. I love Tamar, my brother's sister. What shall
I do?

SERVANT

Is this the reason?

AMNON

You must help me, for I will not be right until something is done.

SERVANT

Hear me out, then. Lay down on your bed and feign yourself sick, and
when your father comes to see you tell him, "Let my sister Tamar come
and give me cakes to eat, and prepare the food in my sight, that I may
see it and eat it at her hand." And surely he will send for her to make
you well, and when she is here I will watch by the door to see that you
are alone with her.

AMNON

Go then, and tell my father I am ill. (*The servant crosses to David, whispers*
to him, and David crosses to Amnon's room.)

DAVID

Amnon, my son.

AMNON

Father, you came.

DAVID

Your servant Yonadav came to me and said, "Your son Amnon is sick
in bed." What ails you?

AMNON

I did not wish to trouble my father.

DAVID

Pray tell me what I may do to make you well.

AMNON

I am gloomy, Father, and my soul lacks cheer. Would that my sister Tamar
came and made her special honeycakes before me, and served them to me
herself. I am feverish, Father, and obsessed with this longing.

PSALMS OF TWO DAVIDS

DAVID

Then I will send for her, that she may cheer your soul.

AMNON

I pray you, Father, think not unkindly of me.

DAVID

My son, this is but a small request.

AMNON

Think not unkindly, or my heart will break.

DAVID

Amnon, Amnon, I am only too glad you sent for me, for I would do anything in my power to make you well.

AMNON

Thank you, Father. I am sure I will be well soon.

DAVID

Then let me hurry now and fetch your sister. (*He leaves and whispers to Tamar. As Tamar crosses to Amnon's room, David stands down right facing front, reacting to the scene which follows but not as if he is overhearing it.*)

TAMAR

Is Amnon awake?

AMNON

Who is it?

TAMAR

Tamar.

AMNON

Come in, I beg of you, that I may see you.

TAMAR

Our father said you were not well.

AMNON

No, Tamar, I am not well.

TAMAR

He said you had a craving for honeycake.

AMNON

Closer, Tamar, I cannot see too clearly.

TAMAR

Shall I make you some cakes, then?

AMNON

Let me look at you first.

TAMAR

I am flattered —

AMNON

Closer.

TAMAR

— that you think so highly —

AMNON

Let me see your face.

TAMAR

— of my baking.

AMNON

Tamar. (*A light comes up on Absalom, who is watching David and reacting to the scene in Amnon's room.*)

TAMAR

Shall I start to prepare them?

AMNON

Do you loathe me?

TAMAR

They will take time to make.

AMNON

Do you detest the sight of me?

TAMAR

They must be kneaded, and they must rise before the baking.

AMNON

Tamar.

TAMAR

Please.

AMNON

(*grabs her wrist*) Come lie with me.

TAMAR

No, my brother, do not force me.

AMNON

Come lie with me!

TAMAR

Do not do this thing! (*He forces her to the floor and forces himself between her legs. The rape continues through the following.*)

DAVID

What have I fathered that would do this thing? Is he a Philistine or Jebusite cur? Has he no sense of God? God! Why do You bring this thing upon my house? Do You try Your servant's faithfulness? I am faithful! I have always been faithful! Think not unkindly, he said to me, think not unkindly or my heart will break! I pray you, Father, he said to me, think not unkindly

182

or my heart will break! What of *my* heart? What is the law? O Lord! (*David dances his anguish as the chorus speaks.*)

CHORUS
David,
son of Jesse the Ephrathite,
king of Israel,
cried, "O Lord! What is the law?"
And he waited
and he listened
and his heart cried,
"David!"

AMNON
How many rules must I break —

CHORUS
Before you'll clasp me to your breast
and say, "I love you anyway,
you are my son"?

DAVID
But I want Absalom!

CHORUS
And David
son of Jesse the Bethlehemite
could raise no hand
against his first son
Amnon.

ABSALOM
But he raped my sister! Why do you bend yourself so to spare and protect him? If I had done this thing, surely you would carry out justice! Do you blame yourself that Amnon is not the heir you want? do you punish yourself for what he has done? Father, be sensible! it is *he* that has committed this sin! (*David exits quickly and Absalom watches after him.*)

AMNON
Get up and be gone.

TAMAR
Amnon, no, don't send me away.

AMNON
Get out, Tamar!

TAMAR
Amnon, hear me: putting me forth like this is as great a wrong as this thing you have forced me to do.

AMNON

Get out!

TAMAR

I will not be defiled and then sent away!

AMNON

Yonadav! Come put this woman out from me and bolt the door after her!
(*She rises and walks from his room, crying out.*)

TAMAR

Israel, see my shame!

ABSALOM

Tamar!

TAMAR

Let the children of Jerusalem spit upon me!

ABSALOM

Tamar!

TAMAR

(*stops and faces him*) I am ruined, Absalom! and as I come now for you
to hide me in your house, let it be known that this is the last day I will
show my shame in the streets of Jerusalem! O Absalom, the air has grown
fetid and the sunlight is cruel! Hide me away where it is dark!

Scene 4

Nathan's house.

NATHAN

Why are you being so obstinate? What keeps you from condemning your
son?

DAVID

My heir.

NATHAN

He should be destroyed.

DAVID

She is only a daughter.

NATHAN

He cannot be king.

DAVID

Is that an order?

NATHAN

God's voice!

DAVID

Or yours?

NATHAN

Do you now take me for a mistaken prophet?

DAVID

I serve the Lord!

NATHAN

You serve your heart! It is only the guilty father of a weakling son that protects this Amnon. Which shall you be: a boy's father or God's servant?

DAVID

How can I be just unless I am each to each?

NATHAN

You must choose!

DAVID

I can't go against my heart!

NATHAN

Then you've chosen.

DAVID

Yes.

NATHAN

(*scowling*) Go in peace.

DAVID

God willing.

NATHAN

That's the question.

Scene 5

The passage of two years.

LEADER

And the moon went into Av
waxed full
waned
and passed into Elul.

CHORUS

(*severally*) Etanim . .
Bul . .
Kislev . .
Tevet . .

Shvat . .
Adar . .
Aviv . .
Ziv . .
    LEADER
And there hung
in the months that followed
an uneasy cloud over Jerusalem
and David the king
did not speak of the matter
and even Absalom did not speak out . .
    CHORUS
(*severally*) Sivan . .
Tammuz . .
Av . .
Elul . .
Etanim . .
Bul . .
Kislev . .
Tevet . .
    LEADER
And gradually
the people forgot
though Tamar was never seen on the streets
and the tension slowly
appeared to dissolve
between the two brothers of David's house . .
    CHORUS
(*severally*) Shvat . .
Adar . .
Aviv . .
Ziv . .
    LEADER
Two years passed
and the harvest came . .
    CHORUS
(*severally*) Sivan . .
Tammuz . .
Av . .
Elul . .

LEADER

And finally Absalom spoke.

ABSALOM

Amnon.

AMNON

My brother.

ABSALOM

The season has come to shear the sheep. I wonder if you would care to join me at my place in Judah for the festival?

AMNON

Join you in Judah?

ABSALOM

For a week or so.

AMNON

Will our father be coming?

ABSALOM

He sends his regrets and begs that Amnon go in his stead, that once again we brothers shall sit and eat at one table. I trust you will come?

AMNON

I will come.

ABSALOM

Good.

LEADER

And Elul passed
and the month was Etanim.

Scene 6

Absalom's country house. To an ominous rhythm, carried over from the last scene, the stage is set for a banquet. Amnon is carried on a litter to the center of the table; Absalom, also on a litter, is brought to the foot of the table; the head of the table is conspicuously vacant. The rhythm continues through the following.

ABSALOM

Well! We are gathered at last at one table. The family is whole again, the brothers reunited, and it seems after some question that the house will stand. Amnon, is something wrong? You seem to be perspiring.

AMNON

It is only the heat of the torches.

JOEL SCHWARTZ

ABSALOM

Good; I was afraid you might be feverish and miss the highlight of the feast. Now that would distress me, as you are the guest of honor, which is why I've asked my servants to surround you so.

AMNON

Excuse me, brother, I did not catch the reason.

ABSALOM

I say, as the guest of honor, you deserve my finest attendants at your beck and call.

AMNON

I am deeply grateful.

ABSALOM

It's the season of gratitude. Even the sheep, though little they realize it now, will no doubt be relieved to have the burden of their fleece lightened on their backs. It is always a mystery to me how they seem to know when their time has come; the restlessness infests the flock, there is that look of panic as they see themselves surrounded by my men. And the fear and the terror in their eyes as they realize how helpless they are, so cornered, so trapped, so much at my mercy. But it is only because the shearing is needed that we can take such delight in subjecting them to the sharpened blades, and no matter how desperately they bleat and beg and cry as if experiencing some abominable pain — Amnon, are you certain that you feel well, my brother?

AMNON

Yes, fine, if I could have a little room to breathe.

ABSALOM

Take no notice of my men; they are only there to serve you. So! let us get on with the feast. But it seems odd to me that no one sits at the head of my table. Does that not seem odd to everyone? Oh yes, now I recall why the place is vacant. I am generally accustomed to having my dearest friend sit there, but I must confess she is shy and of late unused to the presence of so many guests. As a matter of fact, the woman has taken it into her head that she dare not show herself in public. But I could no more feast without her than I could let an assault on her virtue go unchallenged. So: enough has been said. Bring Tamar my sister to the table. (*Tamar is carried in. She has grown fat and ugly during her two years of withdrawal. Amnon is held in his seat by the attendants, who are watching Absalom for a signal.*) Give her some light! bring her a torch! My brother has not seen her in two long years, and I am sure he will want to see the face he once cherished!

PSALMS OF TWO DAVIDS

AMNON

Enough! enough!

ABSALOM

Has Tamar anything to say? (*She shakes her head. Absalom gives the signal, and the attendants slay Amnon. As his body is carried off, and the set is cleared of the banquet table, Absalom and Tamar step down from their litters and cross to each other. He offers his hand, and for a moment they are again a regal couple.*) Close up the house! pack everything! We are quitting Judah and all of Israel! Let a caravan be formed and we will go into the desert! Come, let us muster what dignity we have left! (*As the stage becomes clear of all but Absalom and Tamar, lights come up on David holding the body of Amnon. David looks at Absalom helplessly, as Tamar turns away. Absalom, full of anger, guilt, and pity, cannot find the words he would say to David. Finally he cries out.*) It had to be done!

Scene 7

David's court. Mournful chords on wind instruments fade into a slow, steady rhythm of whole notes. Lights first begin to come up on the edges of the stage, where actors are moving in place in slow motion and chanting softly.

ACTORS

Bul	(*beat*)	Kis-	lev
(*beat*)	(*beat*)	Te-	vet
(*beat*)	(*beat*)	Shvat	(*beat*)
A-	(*beat*)	dar	(*beat*)
A-	viv	(*beat*)	Ziv
Si-	(*beat*)	(*beat*)	van
Ta-	(*beat*)	muz	Av
E-	(*beat*)	tanim	(*beat*)

(*As this repeats, a half-tone higher and slightly louder with each repetition, lights come up on David who sits, alone and dejected, on his throne. Over the actors' voices he chants the following on one note and raises his pitch a half-tone with each repetition.*)

DAVID

Ab-	(*beat*)	(*beat*)	(*beat*)
Ab-	(*beat*)	sa-	(*beat*)
Ab-	sa-	(*beat*)	(*beat*)
Ab-	(*beat*)	salom	(*beat*)
Ab-	(*beat*)	(*beat*)	(*beat*)
sa-	(*beat*)	(*beat*)	lom

189

Ab- (*beat*) Ab- sa-
(*beat*) Ab- sa- (*beat*)
(*After these syllables have been repeated, the wind instruments end with
"official" chords that set the stage as David's court. Yoab, a servant of
David's, calls a woman over to his side.*)

YOAB

I pray you, feign yourself to be a mourner, and put on mourning apparel,
I pray you, and go in to the king and say:

WOMAN

(*covering her head with a shawl*) Help me, O king of Israel.

DAVID

What ails you?

WOMAN

Of truth I am a widow, my husband being dead. And I had two sons,
and they strove together, but the one smote the other and killed him. And,
behold, the whole family has risen up and said, "Deliver him that smote
his brother, that we may kill him also." Thus will they take my son which
is left, and will leave to my husband neither name nor remainder on the
earth.

DAVID

Go to your house, and whoever says anything to you, bring him to me.
As the Lord lives, not one hair of your son shall fall to the earth.

WOMAN

Let your handmaid, I pray you, speak a word to my lord.

DAVID

Say on.

WOMAN

In speaking this word the king is as one that is guilty himself, in that he
does not fetch home his son in exile. For we all must die, and are as water
spilt on the ground which cannot be gathered up again. I pray you, let
he that is banished be not an outcast anymore.

DAVID

Is the hand of my servant Yoab with you in all this?

WOMAN

As your soul lives.

DAVID

Truly now, I grant this request. Go and bring the young man Absalom
back.

YOAB

Today your servant knows he has found favor in your sight.

DAVID

But Yoab, when you fetch Absalom from the wilderness of Geshur, let him turn to his own house, but let him not see my face. (*The court bows and exits, leaving David alone. Absalom enters, and stands at a distance from the king.*)

ABSALOM

Why am I come from Geshur? It were better for me to be there still. Let me see the king's face! and if there be iniquity in me, let him kill me. (*David cannot hold himself back from Absalom, and the two kiss and embrace each other.*)

Scene 8

Nathan's house.

ABSALOM

The winds seem to have shifted in my absence.

NATHAN

As they do before a storm.

ABSALOM

I have heard many things among the people. Is it true my father no longer confides in you?

NATHAN

Yes.

ABSALOM

He always used to.

NATHAN

For a time.

ABSALOM

Nathan, as you see it, do you think David is the man he meant to be?

NATHAN

I think he is tired in spirit and broken in will.

ABSALOM

I had always seen him as a man who would risk everything for greatness, yet I feel he is now overwhelmed by the price and thinks second and third thoughts before daring to act.

NATHAN

The weight of the crown exhausts him.

ABSALOM

Look at him now, Nathan, he is not able to deal with the growing demands of Jerusalem, and the kingdom is desperate for more leadership than he gives. Ten more years and Israel will split apart again, there will be war, the capital will be moved, and Jerusalem will decline in its infancy. Nathan, for Israel's sake these things must not happen, and for David's sake he must never see them.

NATHAN

Have you come to enlist my support?

ABSALOM

I have been feeling the people out and they are mine for the asking. I have some men of my own, but I want no battle, and I think blood can be avoided if we are clever.

NATHAN

You have a plan?

ABSALOM

Yes. And once I have taken the throne and begun to restore the kingdom as my father would want to see it, David and I will be reconciled. I know how painful and how full of misunderstandings it will be at first, but I am certain in time he will understand I have acted only out of love and respect.

NATHAN

I must warn you there is much grief in this path.

ABSALOM

And none if Israel were left to crumble? I have chosen between them, Nathan.

Scene 9

The scheme. A rhythm suggests the tension of waiting. Lights dimly come up on three of Absalom's men, who are scattered around the edges of the stage. They are waiting for a signal and relay phrases to one another.

FIRST MAN

(*sotto voce to second*) Is it time?

SECOND MAN

(*sotto voce to third*) Is it time?

THIRD MAN

(*sotto voce to first*) Not yet.

FIRST MAN

Not yet.

SECOND MAN

Hush.

THIRD MAN

Listen!

FIRST MAN

Nothing.

SECOND MAN

Nothing.

THIRD MAN

Listen — there's rustling!

FIRST MAN

In the bushes!

SECOND MAN

— lizards.

THIRD MAN

A far cry from trumpets.

FIRST MAN

Easy . .

SECOND MAN

Be calm.

FIRST MAN

The signal will come.

THIRD MAN

And if something's happened . .

SECOND MAN

Nothing's happened.

THIRD MAN

. . to Absalom?

FIRST MAN

Nothing.

SECOND MAN

The Lord is with him.

FIRST MAN

The crown is his shield.

THIRD MAN

Not his —

FIRST MAN

Not yet.

SECOND MAN

But shortly.

THIRD MAN

With luck.

FIRST MAN

Listen —

SECOND MAN

Listen —

FIRST MAN

We are not a band of rogues.

SECOND MAN

Nor foolish conspirers.

FIRST MAN

But the will of the people and tools of the Lord.

SECOND MAN

Faith.

FIRST MAN

Faith!

THIRD MAN

Hush! (*Trumpets. The following are proclamations.*)

FIRST MAN

Absalom is king — in Hebron!

SECOND MAN

       Absalom is king — in Hebron!

THIRD MAN

            Absalom is king!

FIRST MAN

Long live Absalom!

SECOND MAN

  Long live Absalom!

THIRD MAN

     Long live Absalom!

FIRST MAN

Listen to the echo!

SECOND MAN

In hours it will sound from Dan to Beersheva!

THIRD MAN

Spread the word!

FIRST MAN

Spread the word! (*Trumpets. The three shift positions, moving further off.*)

FIRST MAN

Absalom is king — in Ashkelon!

SECOND MAN

     Absalom is king — in Ashkelon!

THIRD MAN

Absalom — is king!

FIRST MAN

Long live Absalom!

SECOND MAN

Long live Absalom!

THIRD MAN

Long live Absalom!

(*Trumpets. The three move further off.*)

FIRST MAN

Absalom is king — in Beersheva!

SECOND MAN

Absalom is king — in Beersheva!

THIRD MAN

Absalom — is king!

FIRST MAN

Long live Absalom!

SECOND MAN

Long live Absalom!

THIRD MAN

Long live Absalom!

(*trumpets*)

Scene 10

David's court. David is with a messenger. In the distance they hear the following.

FIRST ACTOR

Absalom is king — in Bethlehem!

SECOND ACTOR

Absalom is king — in Bethlehem!

THIRD ACTOR

Absalom — is king!

FIRST ACTOR

Long live Absalom!

SECOND ACTOR

Long live Absalom!

THIRD ACTOR
Long live Absalom!

DAVID
Is it true what they cry?
MESSENGER
Israel is with him.
DAVID
Even in Bethlehem?
MESSENGER
The cry has been heard.
DAVID
How great are his armies?
MESSENGER
I have not seen them, but they seem to be everywhere.

FIRST ACTOR
(off) In Jericho! — Long live Absalom!
SECOND ACTOR
In Jericho!
THIRD ACTOR
In Jericho!

DAVID
Arise, and let us flee, or else there will be no escape for us from Absalom. We must go in haste, lest he overtake us quickly, and bring down evil upon us, and smite the city with the edge of the sword.
MESSENGER
Shall we go armed?
DAVID
There isn't the time. Wake everyone up!
MESSENGER
Your servants are ready to do the king's bidding.
DAVID
Then let our arms be collected as we gather our things to leave, but with the greatest speed, lest he find us here and make war in Jerusalem.
MESSENGER
The gates are strong.
DAVID
But we will not hide behind them. I will not see an inch of Jerusalem either damaged or upturned, nor a drop of blood upon her streets. I would rather leave Absalom the city, the palace, the throne, and the crown than see war in my city.

PSALMS OF TWO DAVIDS

MESSENGER

It will no longer be your city.

DAVID

Truly, that may be so, and if I never see it again let me only leave it whole as a prize for my son. Hurry, wake the court, we must leave and I must not give even a moment's thought to what is happening. (*The messenger exits.*) Absalom — ! (*stifles the cry*) How will we leave if Jerusalem too is against us? Messenger! (*Another messenger enters.*) What of the men of Jerusalem: do they hail Absalom as king?

MESSENGER

Nothing has been heard.

DAVID

But it won't be long, not more than the night. We must take care to leave at dawn, when the streets are deserted, else we may be stoned for our pains.

MESSENGER

My lord, can you believe in your heart that Jerusalem would ever betray you?

DAVID

There is nothing beyond belief anymore after all that has been! Jerusalem is only the younger of my beloved children — and the elder is marching on me to take all that I have! Not the crown, nor the throne, that's not what he's after! but my heart, what's left of it — the last sinews and muscles that drew their best strength from my love for him! That's what he wants! to rip loose my only roots in the world of men! (*The messenger withdraws.*)
My God, my God, why have You forsaken me?
Why are You so far from helping me, from the words of my distress?
I am a worm and no man,
scorned by men and despised by the people!
All who see me mock me,
they make mouths at me, they wag their heads!
Be not far from me,
for trouble is near
and there is none to help!
Wake up! arise and spread the word we are leaving! the king has abdicated while you slept and dreamt! Rouse yourselves, those who still love David, that we may leave a spotless house! make ready in haste, let us save our necks, for my son has already been lethal with his hands! Come, let's be gone! already I feel the breath of Absalom upon our necks! (*Trumpets. From all parts of the stage members of the court enter carrying hastily*

wrapped bundles.) By now you must all have heard the news. There is rebellion in Israel and Absalom is king. We are leaving Jerusalem, we are leaving everything exactly in place for Absalom's sake; I want no chaos, and above all no war. Let this thing be done in peace and in dignity. The sun is coming up, and by the time it is risen it will find a new Jerusalem, for we will be gone. Let us form a train and pass through the streets leading out to the north. We will keep silence as we walk, we will only look forward, and if there should be people who come out to curse us or throw stones in our path we will lower our heads and not slacken our pace. I will be walking at the head of the train; I will not look back, I will not know who is following me. Anyone who wishes to stay behind and serve my son, I beg you, stay, I will not be offended. So: if we are ready to leave, let those of you who are coming with me form a line behind me, and let the others stay behind to make ready for Absalom. Come, let us go. (*The interior setting is transformed into an exterior scene as a full sunrise unfolds before David's eyes. Gradually all the members of the court fall in behind David, as the king raises his hands in a gesture of giving thanks.*)
O Lord, our Lord,
how excellent is Your name in all the earth!

When I look at Your heavens, the work of Your fingers,
the moon and the stars which You have made,
what is man that You are mindful of him,
and the son of man that You do care for him?

O Lord, our Lord,
how excellent is Your name in all the earth!
(*A servant enters carrying the Ark.*)

    SERVANT

My lord, you cannot mean to leave the Ark behind. Let us bring it with us.

    DAVID

Carry the Ark of God back. If I find favor in the eyes of the Lord, He will bring me back and let me see both it and His dwelling place, but if He says, "I have no pleasure in you," then here I am, let Him do to me what seems good to Him. Come, let us depart for once and for all; there is no good in my tarrying longer. (*Music is heard as the stately recessional begins its way around the stage. As the group is about to exit, a few of the people of Jerusalem emerge and stand in front of them. The recession and the music pause for a tense moment as David braces himself for the people's reaction. Two women with baskets step forward and suddenly begin to wail and strew flowers in David's path. The king is clearly moved. Ittai, one of the townspeople, speaks softly.)*

ITTAI

Stay. (*David, unable to speak, shakes his head.*) Then I will go with you.

DAVID

Shall I make you wander about with us, seeing I go I know not where? Go back, and take your brothers with you, and may the Lord show love and faithfulness to you.

ITTAI

As the Lord lives, and as my lord the king lives, wherever the king shall be, whether for death or for life, there also will your servant be.

DAVID

Come. (*The recession proceeds down from the stage to the nearest exit, with Ittai and a few others joining David's train. The two women with flowers watch after them, as does the servant with the Ark who remained stage center. When the train has exited, the servant slowly carries back the Ark; and the women wearily begin to sweep up the trampled flowers.*)

Scene 11

David's court. The set is dimly lit. David's robe and crown are on the throne. Absalom enters with a torch and looks around. Finally he sees his father's robe, and with great ambivalence he puts it on. As the strain upon him increases, he lifts the crown.

ABSALOM

Bring me wine! We will hold court at once and lay out our plans. (*Lights come up as Absalom's entourage enters. He is brought wine and begins to drink heavily, which he continues to do throughout the scene. Gradually the court is assembled.*) I have come back from my exile to the place where I was raised, and today the House of Israel will give me back the kingdom.

COURTIERS

Long live the king!

ABSALOM

Hushai, come forth. Why is it that you tarried here and hailed me king when you were of my father's court? Is this your loyalty to your friend? Why did you not go with your friend?

HUSHAI

Whom the Lord and this people and all Israel have chosen, his will I be, and with him I will remain. And again, whom should I serve? Should it not be his son? As I have served your father, so I will serve you.

ABSALOM

Ahitophel, give us your counsel; what shall we do?

AHITOPHEL

My lord, go in to your father's concubines whom he has left to keep the house, and all Israel will hear that you have made yourself odious to your father. Thus the hands of all who are with you will be strengthened.

ABSALOM

Do you mock me?

AHITOPHEL

I speak in earnest.

ABSALOM

Truly?

AHITOPHEL

My lord, the moment is critical. Whatever your thoughts may have been before, you have no choice now but to claim your rights as king.

ABSALOM

(*with growing discomfort*) Go on.

AHITOPHEL

Let me choose twelve thousand men, and I will set out and pursue David tonight. I will come upon him while he is weary and discouraged and throw him into a panic, and all the people who are with him will flee. I will strike down the king only, and I will bring all the people back to you as a bride comes home to her husband.

ABSALOM

Let us hear what Hushai has to say.

HUSHAI

My lord, your father is expert in war; he will not spend the night with the people. Surely even now he has hidden himself in one of the pits, or in some other place. My counsel is that you go to battle in person. So we shall come upon him in some place where he is to be found, and we shall light upon him as the dew falls on the ground; and of him and all his men with him not one will be left.

ABSALOM

Is there no way to spare David?

HUSHAI

My lord, there cannot be two kings in one Israel.

ABSALOM

(*feeling a depression rising within him*) Let us sleep tonight, and tomorrow we will dress for battle. The counsel of Hushai is better. (*The drums of battle are heard.*)

Scene 12

The battle between David and Absalom. Drums and trumpets as the lights come up. Three actors, holding open libretti, read the following in concert fashion.

FIRST ACTOR
Da-vid (*drum*) the fa- ther (*drum*) (*drum*)
SECOND ACTOR
                     Da- vid   the
THIRD ACTOR
Da-vid

FIRST ACTOR
Da-vid (*drum*) the (*drum*)   the
SECOND ACTOR
Da-vid   the
THIRD ACTOR
                    the king!

FIRST ACTOR
Da-vid (*drum*)   (*drum*)
SECOND ACTOR
Da-vid
THIRD ACTOR
           the bat- tle   of

FIRST ACTOR
Da-vid (*drum*) the fa- ther
SECOND ACTOR
    Da- vid
THIRD ACTOR
         Ab- sa- lom!

(*A soldier appears up right doing the spear-carrier dance; two more enter down left doing the dance. When the three meet at center, the second and third lunge; the first stiffens, pivots, falls backward into their hands and is dragged off. During the following, several actors creep up around the edges of the stage.*)

FIRST ACTOR

Da-vid (*drum*) the king!   (*drum*)

SECOND ACTOR

Da-vid   the   king!

THIRD ACTOR

the king   a- gainst the   king!

(*Hushai enters furtively and approaches a group of actors.*)

HUSHAI

Can you get a message to David?

SOLDIER

He's waiting to hear from you.

HUSHAI

Then send quickly and tell him: ''Thus and thus have I counseled Absalom. Do not lodge tonight in the plains of the wilderness but instead pass over, lest the king be swallowed up and all the people that are with him.''

SOLDIER

I will give him the message. (*Hushai and the soldier withdraw to different sides of the stage.*)

FIRST ACTOR

Da-vid   and

SECOND ACTOR

Da- vid

THIRD ACTOR

and Ab- sa- lom

FIRST ACTOR

the king   a- gainst

SECOND ACTOR

the king   the   king!

THIRD ACTOR

the   king   the   king!

(*They put down the libretti and join the other actors as trumpets sound. David enters, carried on the shoulders of two soldiers.*)

DAVID

Rise up and pass quickly over the Jordan! By dawn we must all be across the river, for Hushai has sent word what he counseled Absalom! (*David and his men, up left, mime wading through the river. Absalom enters down right, carried on the shoulders of two soldiers. He and his men do not see David's entourage.*)

PSALMS OF TWO DAVIDS

ABSALOM

Make haste, we must cross the Jordan to chase them! They passed over this morning and can't be far! (*Absalom and his men, down right, mime wading through the river. Although both groups are virtually moving toward each other, they do not see one another.*)

DAVID

Here will be our camp, but I will go forth in battle with you myself.

ITTAI

Do not go forth. If we flee away they will not care for us, nor if half of us die will it mean a thing; but you are worth ten thousand of us, thus it is better that you stay.

DAVID

Whatever seems best to you I will do. (*touches his shoulder*) But deal gently for my sake with the young man Absalom.

ABSALOM

Let us search the land for David's men, and let the first who finds them send word at once! (*David and Absalom are lowered at the same rhythm. David's men begin, with stylized movement and a percussion background, crawling through woods. Absalom's men, also in stylized movement, search for David's men. One of them cries out.*)

SOLDIER

His men are passing through Gilead!

DAVID

(*standing on the highest platform, up left*)
I lay me down, and I sleep;
I awake, for the Lord sustains me.
I am not afraid of ten thousands of people
that have set themselves against me round about!

ANOTHER SOLDIER

His men are in Mahanaim!

DAVID

Be gracious unto me, O God, be gracious unto me,
for in You my soul takes refuge;
yea, in the shadow of Your wings will I take refuge
till the storms of destruction pass!

ANOTHER SOLDIER

They are deep in the forest of Ephraim! (*During the following, young David from Part One enters unseen and watches the king.*)

KING DAVID

O Lord, how many are my foes!

Many are rising up against me!
Many are . .
YOUNG DAVID
(*recognizing the words and overlapping*)
. . many are saying of me,
there is no help for him in God.
O Lord, how many are my foes!
(*King David has been watching young David as if seeing a vision; the two
stare at each other.*)
ABSALOM
(*to his men*) Come, I will go with you into the forest. (*As Absalom's and
David's men creep offstage, Nathan is carried in on a litter between the
two Davids.*)
KING DAVID
Nathan! why is life so cruel that I must always fight the person I love?
NATHAN
Ask yourself!
KING DAVID
But why my son Absalom? Why is it Absalom? Had it been Amnon my
heart would not be breaking!
NATHAN
You once had Amnon set against you, but you pitied his weakness and
dared not act.
KING DAVID
Would that I could relive that day, for Absalom has never forgiven me!
If only I had known it would come to this! (*A messenger rushes in to the
edge of the stage.*)
MESSENGER
My lord!
KING DAVID
What is it?
MESSENGER
News of the battle!
KING DAVID
Give me the word!
MESSENGER
The day is yours!
KING DAVID
But what of the young man Absalom? (*A tense rhythm begins to build.*)
Is it well with the young man Absalom?

PSALMS OF TWO DAVIDS

MESSENGER

It is said —

KING DAVID

Deal gently! Those were my words!

MESSENGER

The order was given . .

KING DAVID

Then he was not slain!

MESSENGER

Not slain, my lord . .

KING DAVID

Thank God he lives!

MESSENGER

The Lord have mercy.

KING DAVID

Why do you mumble? Was Absalom hurt?

MESSENGER

My lord —

KING DAVID

Tell me!

MESSENGER

They say he was riding through the thickest part of the forest —

KING DAVID

Yes?

MESSENGER

And the low branches caught his hair, and his horse continued to run —

KING DAVID

Yes?

MESSENGER

And there he was found.

KING DAVID

There —? found —? hanging —? (*pause*) Was there any breath?

MESSENGER

He was dead. (*The messenger withdraws.*)

KING DAVID

(*cries out*) O my son Absalom! my son, my son Absalom! would I had died for you, O Absalom! my son, my son!

YOUNG DAVID

(*to Nathan*) Samuel! enough of these visions! Show me no more than I have seen!

NATHAN

(*as he is carried off*) You asked for the outcome. Look!

YOUNG DAVID

Don't go! I only wanted to know about Jonathan! (*Both Davids are left alone on stage.*)

KING DAVID

O Israel, your glory is slain on high!
How are the mighty fallen!

YOUNG DAVID

No!

KING DAVID

(*seeing young David*) It will be!

YOUNG DAVID

God spare!

KING DAVID

God spare? do you think so? Well, there's an interesting problem for my philosophers. Wrong! Philosophers!

YOUNG DAVID

I will not go mad!

KING DAVID

Not even after what you have seen?

YOUNG DAVID

The Lord will protect me!

KING DAVID

Protect yourself!

YOUNG DAVID

I will serve His will!

KING DAVID

Then use your own!

YOUNG DAVID

No! That is no way to serve the Lord!

KING DAVID

It's the only way!

YOUNG DAVID

How can you say that?

KING DAVID

Look how I failed to act with Amnon and waited for the Lord to act! Learn from my mistake!

YOUNG DAVID

All right! I will act when the moment comes!

PSALMS OF TWO DAVIDS

KING DAVID

Child, the moment *has* come! Listen to Samuel! Look — he told you the kingdom is yours! Why are you waiting?

YOUNG DAVID

I —

KING DAVID

Are you waiting for Jonathan's blood to be shed?

YOUNG DAVID

But that — that's a different matter!

KING DAVID

No! it's the same! it's up to you and the choice is yours!

YOUNG DAVID

The choice is the Lord's!

KING DAVID

The Lord only judges the choice you make!

YOUNG DAVID

But —

KING DAVID

There is no one else to blame! David, your life is the work of your hand!

YOUNG DAVID

Is it up to me?

KING DAVID

Always! David, make your choice! Act now! Don't wait!

YOUNG DAVID

(*with great effort*) I will — I will try — !

KING DAVID

And praise the Lord!
praise Him with trumpets!
with lutes and harps!
with timbrel and dance!
(*Young David joins him.*)

BOTH DAVIDS

And praise Him with the strings and the pipe!
with sounding cymbals!
with loud clashing cymbals!
let everything that breathes praise the Lord!
praise the Lord!

THE END

JOEL SCHWARTZ

Psalms of Two Davids by Joel Schwartz was presented May 7–15, 1971, at the College of Marin, Kentfield, California. It was directed by James Dunn.

Cast of Characters

SAMUEL	Reynold Acevedo
KING SAUL	Gregory Norgaard
JONATHAN	John Evans
MICHAL	Pamela Contos
DAVID (as a young man)	Joel Blum
NATHAN	Reynold Acevedo
KING DAVID	Mark Rasmussen
ABSALOM	John Evans
TAMAR	Pamela Contos
AMNON	Robin Williams
CHORUS	Rick Casorla, J. W. Harper, Shelly Lipkin, Howard McMaster, Denise Orr, Alice Rorvik, H. J. Susser, Roxane Wilkinson
SOLDIERS	John Chapot, Alan Monroe, Todd Norris, Louis Parnell, Ernie Shelton, Reg Woods